Your Guide to Amazon Suspensions

Your Guide to Amazon Suspensions

2017-2018 Edition

CJ Rosenbaum

Purpose of this Book

We help suspended sellers get their Amazon accounts reinstated. Unlike many lawyers, we do not want any of our clients involved in litigation. We help suspended sellers obtain reinstatement as quickly as possible.

There are two main goals of this book:

- Educate Amazon sellers about how to avoid suspensions.
- Teach suspended Amazon sellers how to get their accounts reinstated.

Prologue to *Sellers: Stop Living in Fear*

Stop living in fear. This book is written to empower Amazon sellers. The information now in your hands comes from reinstating sellers around the world. Use what we have learned to maintain your selling privileges, and if you receive the dreaded suspension e-mail, use this book to carry you to your quick reinstatement.

Having met thousands of Amazon sellers around the world, the common thread is that you live in fear of your account being suspended. Small sellers fear not being able to pay their bills or maintain their lifestyles. Those with large accounts fear not being able to make payroll.

Many people think that lawyers are only meant for litigation. This is wrong. A business lawyer's job is to help you continue to do business. If a lawyer is leading you directly to the courthouse on a business matter, that lawyer may be influenced by his or her interest in earning litigation fees. Business matters are overwhelmingly better handled by avoiding the courthouse. Litigation generates fees for lawyers; litigation does not make sense for most businesses.

While I have heard "I want to sue Amazon for doing this to me!" from suspended Amazon sellers more times than I can count, it is generally the wrong way to look at the challenges Amazon throws at its sellers.

Negative Facts about Amazon and Sellers:

- Amazon focuses on customers, not sellers. Sellers are replaceable. Large or small, Amazon is incredibly diversified with sellers. It seems that no individual account, large or small, is, by itself, important to Amazon.
- All sellers live in fear of being suspended.
- Amazon insists on a practically perfect business execution.

Great Facts about Amazon and Sellers:

- You have access to eighty million customers. At no time in the history of commerce have people and businesses had the opportunity that Amazon provides. Even with all the obstacles and callousness toward sellers, Amazon provides one of the greatest opportunities in the history of retail.
- If you have a smartphone and a credit card, you can go into business and compete with the big boys.

With great opportunity comes great challenges. You want to play on their field, Amazon reserves the right to suspend your seller's account with no notice and hold your money. Unlike every other landlord in the United States, Amazon can kick you out of your virtual store at any point in time.

By becoming an Amazon Seller, you agreed to their deal. You agreed that Amazon can suspend you, kick you out, hold your money, and impose innumerable fees on your account. You agreed that Amazon can change the rules whenever it wants. You agreed that if there was a dispute with their incredibly one-sided agreement or any other aspect of doing business on the Amazon platform, you will resolve the issues via arbitration and not use the court system. You agreed not to sue Amazon.

This book is intended to teach you how to work within Amazon's system to get your listing or your account back online after a suspension.

In the chapters to come, we will provide you information about the following:

- Basic Types of Suspensions
- Most Common Reasons for Suspensions
- Basic Method for Reinstatement of Selling Privileges: the POA
- Time Limit for Submitting POA
- Basic Format of POA
- Information on Submitting Your POA to Amazon
- What You Can Expect in Response to Your POA from Amazon
- How to Handle Requests for More Information from Amazon after Submitting Your Initial POA.

CJ Rosenbaum, Esq., Author, Partner Rosenbaum Famularo, P.C., the law firm behind AmazonSellersLawyer.com

Nicole Kulaga, Contributing Editor, Future Lawyer

I began representing Amazon Sellers when a close friend and client called me in a panic. She had recently purchased an interest in a business where Amazon sales were vital. The business' account was suspended. She wanted my help due to my experience as an entrepreneurs' lawyer. I had successfully litigated against corporate giants including Wal-Mart, McDonalds, Sears, KFC, AIG, and other tremendous insurance companies and numerous municipalities. I looked for someone to help. I researched the available resources.

I found that Amazon sellers had no law firms focused on their specific needs. Sellers were either using "Amazon Account Consultants," buying forms online that did not pertain to their specific issues or address their specific accounts. There was no law firm with any significant presence available to stand with suspended Amazon sellers.

I decided that Amazon sellers should have a law firm to stand with them. I created a website for this area of practice that is now known around the world:

AmazonSellersLawyer.com.

My law firm, Rosenbaum Famularo, P.C., focuses on the needs of Amazon sellers. We have lawyers, paralegals, former Amazon sellers, and others on staff around the world. Our clients have the opportunity to meet with us, in person, at locations in New York, San Francisco, Seattle, London, Dublin, Shenzhen, and now Mumbai.

Amazon sellers are not alone anymore.

Since focusing my law firm on the needs of Amazon Sellers, we have successfully reinstated countless accounts, obtained retractions of practically every intellectual property complaint we have worked on, and resolved many issues with Amazon's staff in the United States, India, Ireland, Costa Rica, and the United Kingdom. I am regularly in touch with the top lawyers who represent Amazon and speak at Amazon seller events around the world.

As far as I am aware, there is no other law firm in the world that handles as many Amazon suspensions as we do.

Unlike the "Amazon Suspension Consultants" and websites that claim they can help suspended Amazon sellers, at my law firm

- every document is either drafted by a lawyer or reviewed by a lawyer;
- all the people who work on your suspended accounts are college-educated Americans; we do not outsource anything having to do with your seller's account to anyone in the Philippines or anywhere else;
- we have a centralized location. All of your Plans of Action and other documents are written in New York. We do not use anyone outside of our law firm to work on your account; and
- every Plan of Action is discussed among our team to make sure that we are making the best arguments for your reinstatement.

Our War Room led by Anthony Famularo, Esq., (far right) a partner with the firm, where every Plan of Action is conferenced among our team.

My belief system and philosophy on helping Amazon sellers: our job is to get you back to business, back online, and back making money.

Our job is not to blindly follow Amazon's policies, especially ones that I think are bad for sellers. Our job is to help you get back online, provide you with advice so that you can make business decisions based upon risk versus reward, and to help you accomplish your goals.

My law firm represents our clients, not Amazon. We help Amazon sellers.

In addition to helping sellers with suspensions, this book discusses topics that are clearly against Amazon's policies:

- Maintaining multiple accounts
- New or "Ghost" accounts for those who cannot obtain reinstatement
- Buying and selling Amazon accounts without losing rankings and reviews

If you are a glutton for data or want specific information about the sale of specific lines of products, we currently have two other books available…on Amazon:

Amazon Law Library, Volume 1,
a compilation and summary of hundreds of lawsuits,
where Amazon either sued or was sued

&

Your Guide to Selling Fashion on Amazon.

Legal Disclaimer

This book is designed to provide educational information about how to run an Amazon account and handle suspension issues that may arise. The content of this book is the sole expression and opinion of the authors. The authors and publisher are not offering this book as legal, accounting, or other professional advice. The authors and publisher make no representations or warranties of any kind and assume no liabilities of any kind with respect to the accuracy or completeness of this book's contents. Further, the authors and publisher specifically disclaim any implied warranties of merchantability or fitness of use for a particulate purpose.

Neither the authors nor the publisher shall be liable for any physical, psychological, emotional, financial, or commercial damages, including but not limited to, special, incidental, consequential, or other damages. Neither the authors nor publisher shall be held liable to any person or entity with respect to any loss or incidental or consequential damages caused, or alleged to have been caused, directly or indirectly, by the information or content provided within this book.

This book is intended to serve as a reference—you are responsible for your own choices, actions, and results.

Contents

One

Basics on Suspensions and Getting Back Online

BASIC TYPES OF SUSPENSIONS:

There are two basic types of suspension: listing suspensions and account suspensions.

A listing suspension is where you have been prevented from selling a single product, type of product, or brand of product. But, fortunately, the balance of your account is still active. You are still selling products on Amazon and making money. You might be making less money without the suspended listings, but your business is still open and your payments are still coming to you. This is, of course, better than having your entire account suspended.

When your account was suspended, you received the dreaded e-mail that stated, "Your selling privileges have been suspended." You cannot sell anything to anyone on this account (yes, many people have multiple accounts despite Amazon's prohibition against having more than one account without Amazon's permission.)

When your entire account is suspended, not only are you unable to make any sales but also Amazon withholds your money earned through sales before your suspension. You get hit hard: you cannot earn any money, and Amazon refuses to release money you already earned. You may also suffer:

- storage fees;
- note payments due to Amazon for loans you may have accepted;
- your vendors still need to be paid;
- your employees all still need to be paid; and
- if you are using FBA, you cannot simply sell your products elsewhere, because they are in Amazon's warehouses.

MOST COMMON REASONS FOR SUSPENSIONS

While the specifics of the most common causes of suspensions are discussed in detail in the coming chapters, at my law firm, we see the following as the most common reasons for suspensions:

- Inauthentic (this is different from being accused of selling fake or counterfeit products)
- Used sold as new
- Accusations that you violated someone's or some company's intellectual property rights

BASIC METHOD FOR REINSTATEMENT OF SELLING PRIVILEGES: THE POA

In order to get your listing or account back online, you need to submit a "Plan of Action." We refer to this correspondence as a "POA." A POA is nothing more than an exercise in persuasive writing. You are trying to persuade the reader at Amazon to reinstate your listing or account. In this book, you will learn how to draft a POA.

CJ's Side Note

Plans of Action generally need three sections to work: root cause of the issue, immediate fix to the issue and long-term correction to the business to prevent the issue from occurring again. The problem is that when a seller is suspended, he or she will say whatever it takes to get reinstated. This includes creating "root causes" of the problem when the issue had nothing to do with the product and, instead, the "root cause" of the problem was a customer that wants to scam a free product.

TIME LIMIT FOR SUBMITTING POA

Amazon places a seventeen (17) day time limit—what lawyers call a Statute of Limitations—on providing a POA. Make sure you send something in within seventeen (17) days of receiving your suspension e-mail.

BREAKING NEWS: In July 2017, as this book was being finished, there was news reported that Amazon was going to hold Amazon Sellers to a seven (7) day deadline to respond to Amazon's latest challenge to sellers. Ed Rosenberg wrote in his Facebook group ASGTG.com the following:

> "Important! If you receive a product quality email asking for a plan on an ASIN to avoid suspension of your account, you need to respond even if you're ditching that ASIN. They say in the note that if you do not respond within seven days, you may lose your selling privileges. This is exactly what has been happening. Make sure to respond to those emails with a plan. If you wait one minute before the seven days are up, that may be too late as the POA may not be reviewed in time."

BASIC FORMAT OF POA

There is a basic three-section format for drafting your POA:

1. Root Cause or Causes of the Issue
2. Immediate Corrective Actions
3. Long-Term Business Changes to prevent the issue or problem from reoccurring, also called "Systemic Changes to Business."

The "root causes" of the issues that resulted in your suspension are basically what you identify as the reason for the customer's, Amazon's, a competitor's, or a rights owner's complaint. You need to come up with your own root cause. Amazon doesn't always share with you the underlying issue with your account.

Years ago, it was commonly believed that sellers should always admit to doing something wrong. Many sellers and consultants still suggest that a seller should admit to some wrongdoing even if they did nothing wrong. We do not agree. We do not believe that sellers should admit to wrongdoing if they did nothing wrong or if Amazon is unaware of a seller's policy violations.

Basically, instead of admitting wrongdoing, we suggest that suspended sellers provide Amazon with a method of doing a better job as a seller. The difference is in the verbiage. The importance of not admitting to fault is addressed later in this book.

The "Immediate Corrective Action" section refers to what you already did to remedy the particular issue. Maybe you refunded the customer and sent them another product for free. Maybe you hired staff to help with the issue. You need to provide Amazon with an immediate fix that was intended to make that customer happier.

The long-term changes or systemic changes to your business refers to the alterations to your entire operation that you made or are in the process of making that will prevent similar issues in the future.

BASIC SUBMISSION OF POA TO AMAZON

You can submit your POA to Amazon through a button on your dashboard or e-mail it to the Amazon department that sent you the suspension notice. Most often, your suspension notice came from Seller Performance, which is referred to as "SP," or Product Quality or "PQ."

WHAT YOU CAN EXPECT IN RESPONSE TO YOUR POA

In response to your POA, you can expect one of three e-mails:

1. A request for more information. This is a very common response to an initial POA.
2. An e-mail reinstating your listing or account (this is also very common).
3. An e-mail stating that Amazon is not reinstating your selling privileges (don't despair yet, you can submit countless additional submissions, appeal to a Policy Team, write to the Jeff Bezos' team and, in some circumstances, go to the legal department).

HOW TO HANDLE REQUESTS FOR MORE INFORMATION

When Amazon requests more information, the notice usually comes in one of two forms: a request for specific information or a mind-boggling and frustrating request for all the information you already provided.

When you receive a request for specific information, you should simply provide the information requested: no more, no less.

When you receive a request for the same information you already sent in, the information needs to be reworded, reorganized, better supported by documents, or you may want to hire a lawyer with experience with Amazon to rewrite the POA for you.

POAs are like tax returns: you can do them yourselves, but lawyers who draft them every day may do it better than you.

Two

Why Does Amazon Suspend Accounts

I n order to identify why Amazon suspends sellers, we must under-stand how Amazon thinks and operates. Amazon created the Fourteen Leadership Principles that are ingrained into their operations. While sellers should review all of Amazon's Fourteen Leadership Principals, only the specific Leadership Principals that should be cited in Plans of Action are discussed.

AMAZON'S NUMBER-ONE LEADERSHIP PRINCIPLE: *CUSTOMER OBSESSION*

"Leaders start with the customer and work backwards. They work vigor-ously to earn and keep customer trust. Although leaders pay attention to competitors, they obsess over customers."

The Customer Obsession leadership principle is the driving force behind Amazon's business model. This principal seems to be behind Amazon's incredible growth. Amazon's customer obsession is behind ev-erything the behemoth does. Every time they suspend a seller, it is under the guise of protecting the customers' future experiences.

By obsessing about the customer experience and casting all other issues aside, Amazon has become the most trusted brand on earth.

Customer obsession is why Amazon sellers must be nearly perfect and why Amazon seems to fiercely punish sellers who make mistakes. If you are perfect, the customer obsession is upheld. If you are punished severely for slight infractions or in many cases baseless complaints, other customers will not experience issues and other sellers will work harder to stay in line.

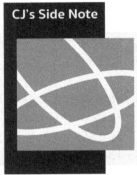

CJ's Side Note

If Customers are #1, What Are Sellers?
Since customers are what Amazon obsesses over, what importance do sellers have to Amazon? If you are asking this question, you are likely relatively new to Amazon. Sellers are replaceable. Sellers do not matter because there are 10 or hundred or more sellers to take your place. Sellers, large and small, all seem to know that they are meaningless and valueless to Amazon. Sellers are not customers.

Amazon's customer obsession supports its tendency to take the customers' side in just about every dispute. If a customer complains about a product, it's a mark against the seller—even if there was nothing wrong.

CJ's Side Note

I have heard people speak about customers being held accountable for abusing the returns policy or other conduct, but I have personally never seen or heard of a buyer being suspended…. neither have any of the attorneys that work for my law firm, lawyers that I work with that represent big brands or any of my staff, family or friends. Even my father who, despite my requests to stop, regularly buys three sizes of all items with the plan of returning two of them, has never received any notice from Amazon about his excessive returns. Dad - please stop hurting sellers.

If there is a complaint about a product having some defect, the seller is required to provide a Plan of Action detailing what he or she did or failed to do to prevent the issue. The first thing sellers should learn from this book is that if there is a complaint, identify what you can do to make the business better, what can be changed so that Amazon's customers do not have the same issue in the future—even where there was never a real problem.

CJ's Side Note

Plans of Action generally need three sections to work: root cause of the issue, immediate fix to the issue and long-term correction to the business to prevent the issue from occurring again. The problem is that when a seller is suspended, he or she will say whatever it takes to get reinstated. This includes creating "root causes" of the problem when the issue had nothing to do with the product and, instead, the "root cause" of the problem was a customer that wants to scam a free product.

AMAZON LEADERSHIP PRINCIPLE: *OWNERSHIP*

"Leaders are owners. They think long term and don't sacrifice long-term value for short-term results. They act on behalf of the entire company, beyond just their own team. They never say 'that's not my job.'"

This "leadership principle" seems to play a role in suspensions because in order to obtain reinstatement, you must accept responsibility for the issue, whether you believe it exists or not. For example, if your account is suspended for "inauthentic" or "used sold as new" or any other category, you need to find an internal reason for the suspension. When a listing or your account is suspended for "inauthentic" you must take responsibility or "own" the responsibility for choosing your suppliers when you submit the invoices that show where you purchased your products. If your listing or account was suspended for "used sold as new," you need to find something with your business that caused the complaint, like poor packaging, that resulted in a customer receiving a damaged product that the customer perceived as used. Then, instead of admitting to a failure, identify a method of avoiding the problem in the future. Make your process, products, and so on, better for Amazon's next customer who receives your goods.

LEARN AND BE CURIOUS
"Leaders are never done learning and always seek to improve themselves. They are curious about new possibilities and act to explore them."

Amazon expects their sellers to remain up to date on all their new policies. If you fail to maintain your account with the new policies, you will be at risk for suspension. It is your job to make sure you know what the rules are and to follow them. There have been times where there have been updates that the seller was not aware of, or didn't pay attention to, that resulted in a suspension. Pay attention.

This principle also plays a role in your "Long Term" or "Systemic Changes to Your Business" portion of your Plans of Action. You should always, as a business practice, be eager to find new ways to improve your business. If you are suspended, that means you must not only follow this principle but also actually demonstrate how you have followed this principle. Show that you have explored new possibilities of improving your business.

HIRE AND DEVELOP THE BEST
"Leaders raise the performance bar with every hire and promotion. They recognize exceptional talent, and willingly move them throughout the organization. Leaders develop leaders and take seriously their role in coaching others. We work on behalf of our people to invent mechanisms for development like Career Choice."

This principle comes into play when writing your "Long Term" or "Systemic Changes to Your Business" section within your Plan of Action. You should demonstrate that you are hiring the best people to work within your business. Sometimes, this requires hiring extra personnel to review all of your invoices, to double check that your listings 100 percent match the items they describe, or to make sure all the packaging is intact when the product arrives at the customer's door. Show Amazon that perfection is a goal your business aims to achieve. Do as Amazon does: achieve better customer satisfaction by hiring the best people you can find.

AMAZON LEADERSHIP PRINCIPLE: *INSIST ON THE HIGHEST STANDARDS*

"Leaders have relentlessly high standards—many people may think these standards are unreasonably high. Leaders are continually raising the bar and driving their teams to deliver high quality products, services and processes. Leaders ensure that defects do not get sent down the line and that problems are fixed so they stay fixed."

Similar to the "ownership" principle, insisting on higher standards also plays a role in your Plans of Action and reinstatement. When there is any suspension of a product or your account, your Plan of Action must describe how your already well-run business run even better. You must show Amazon changes, short and long term, that will prevent similar problems in the future.

AMAZON LEADERSHIP PRINCIPLE: *EARN TRUST*

"Leaders listen attentively, speak candidly, and treat others respectfully. They are vocally self-critical, even when doing so is awkward or embarrassing. Leaders do not believe their or their team's body odor smells of perfume. They benchmark themselves and their teams against the best."

The "Earn Trust" principle seems to be how Amazon's people read your Plans of Action. Plans of Action should be candid, concise, and persuasive.

- In order to "listen attentively," listen or, more accurately, read the suspension notice "attentively" and respond to what the notice seeks. Do not provide extraneous information. Just provide what is sought.
- When it comes to your POA, "speak candidly" means that you should describe clearly what the problem was with your business.

If your staff failed to package your product correctly, say so. If you need more staff to compare your product to the listings or someone to double check your photographs, admit to it and say it concisely.

- "Treating others respectfully," means that your Plan of Action should not insult anyone, especially the customer. Even if you think the issue is entirely the result of a customer trying to scam free merchandise, don't express that in your POA. Your POA must match Amazon's "respect" for each and every customer. That means not blaming the customer for anything. I also think that "treating others respectfully" means that you should never write anything bad about whomever might be reading your POA. For example, you might feel strongly that people in India earning $500 per month should not be deciding the fate of your multimillion-dollar Amazon business. It would be very foolish to write anything that reflects those feelings in your POA. Treat the reader of your POA and all customers with respect...whether you mean it or not.

CJ's Side Note

Your POA is nothing more than an exercise in persuasive writing. You are trying to convince the Amazon staff in India, Costa Rica or Ireland to reinstate your account. Do not insult the person who you want to persuade. Do not insult Amazon in your POA. This seems simple but, I cannot count the number of times my law firm was retained after the seller submitted POAs on their own that were insulting or demeaned the reader or Amazon. Remember the goal of your POA: convince the reader at Amazon to reinstate your listing or account. Remember that "you catch more flies with honey than vinegar." Also, make your POA concise. People from India have confirmed that the staff in India that are reading your POAs have minutes to review your POA and decide to either: reinstate, request more information or deny. You need to convince them to reinstate quickly.

AMAZON LEADERSHIP PRINCIPLE: *DIVE DEEP*

"Leaders operate at all levels, stay connected to the details, audit frequently, and are skeptical when metrics and anecdote differ. No task is beneath them."

When it comes to POAs and obtaining reinstatement, "dive deep" means that the seller thoroughly investigates whatever issue brought to the seller's attention. When you decide what you are going to blame the issue on, state in a few words that you identified the "root cause" of the problem by "diving deep" into your business activities. State to Amazon that you followed their principle. Use the words that Amazon used to train the reader of your POA.

Your deep-dive analysis of your own business can also include the owner of the business getting into the nuts and bolts of the business. Amazon's mantra about there being "no tasks beneath…" anyone is important. The owner of the account should have no problem reviewing the shipping department. If getting into the details is OK for Jeff Bezos, it's OK for you to make sure that your packaging is sufficient.

AMAZON LEADERSHIP PRINCIPLE: *DELIVER RESULTS*

"Leaders focus on the key inputs for their business and deliver them with the right quality and in a timely fashion. Despite setbacks, they rise to the occasion and never settle."

Working this Leadership Principle into the verbiage of your POA. It is easy. All you need to do to mimic this ideal is to use Amazon's words. The reader will recognize the key words because these key words and phrases are essential to working at Amazon: they were part of Amazon's training. Let the reader know that the changes you already made to your business changed the "key inputs" of your operation so that all customers receive "right quality" products "in a timely fashion." That "despite the setbacks," you or your staff are rising to the need of providing better "customer experiences" and that you "will never settle" for anything less than perfect customer experiences.

Keep your goal in mind: persuade the reader at Amazon to reinstate your listing or account. To persuade the reader, use the words and principles you know they are looking for.

CJ's Side Note

A New Orleans lawyer that had a profound effect on my career told me years ago that "it is easier to ride the horse in the direction that it is going." This means that you should give the reader of your POA what they want. Write your POA in their direction they are already going. If you want to sell on Amazon's platform, you need to go with their flow: give the decision makers what they are trained to look for. You don't have to actually believe in Amazon's principles, just get yourself back in business.

If you have been suspended and want to draft your own "Plan of Action," you need to know what Amazon's staff is looking for in your Plan of Action: are you providing the information Amazon wants? Amazon's staff in the United States, India, Ireland, and Costa Rica are trained on Amazon's Leadership Principles. When they read your Plan of Action, reinforce what they already know.

Plans of Action used to be mostly read by people in Seattle. Now, they are mostly read by people in India, in cities called Bangalore and Hyderabad. They are also often read by people in Ireland and Costa Rica and, from time to time, the United States and other locations.

In addition to the Fourteen Leadership Principles, sellers must also recognize that Amazon considers all its customers to be its own customers, and not your customers. What does this mean to Amazon sellers?

Amazon was built on what it calls its Customer Obsession. Start with the customer and work backward. Love Amazon or hate Amazon—their plan worked. Amazon is likely the most recognized and, more importantly, Amazon is likely the most trusted brand in the world.

This is important to sellers because practically all suspensions arise from what causes or might cause a problem for Amazon's customers.

Equally vital to sellers is that you recognize when contacting Amazon that you recognize the "ownership" and bow to it: do not claim or write that you are doing a great job or service to "your" customers. Amazon trains its staff, in the United States and abroad, that the customers are its own customers, and not yours.

CJ's Side Note

If Customers are #1, What Are Sellers?
Since customers are what Amazon obsesses over, what importance do sellers have to Amazon? If you are asking this question, you are likely relatively new to Amazon. Sellers are replaceable. Sellers do not matter because there are 10 or hundred or more sellers to take your place. Sellers, large and small, all seem to know that they are meaningless and valueless to Amazon. Sellers are not customers.

Amazon's obsession with its' customers result in sellers being held to extremely high expectations and requirements.

Common Issues in Retail	Traditional Retail	Amazon
Returns	10–20 percent	Under 10%, varies depending on category
Intellectual Property Issues	If there was any alleged infringement, the complaining party had to go to court and convince a judge that there was some infringement before a traditional retailer was directed to stop selling any particular product.	Upon any complaint, any seller can suffer a suspension of all their selling privileges or be prevented from selling that product. Amazon then compels the retailer to obtain the retraction of the complaint.
Changing Locations	Rent a store from any landlord.	Amazon controls 50 percent of every dollar spent online in the United States. There is no comparable space from which to conduct business in the United States.

We all start businesses to make money, obtain freedom, and achieve success. To be successful, we need to check our performance regularly and track and correct our errors.

The same issues apply to selling on the Amazon platform. In order to satisfy its customers, keep its business running smoothly, and to help sellers remain successful, Amazon has set certain goals or "metrics" that it requires sellers to abide by in order to continue exercising their privilege of selling on the Amazon platform. Amazon created its Seller Performance team for the purpose of evaluating whether sellers on the platform are meeting their requirements of metrics set by Amazon.

Amazon broadly classifies its goals or metrics for sellers as follows:

- Order Defect Rate
- Late Shipment Rate
- Cancellation Rate
- Policies related to trading through Amazon.com

WHAT IS AN ORDER DEFECT RATE?
When an order has been shipped out from the seller's inventory to the customer, and the product receives either negative feedback, an A-to-Z Guarantee Claim, or a Service Credit Chargeback, then the product is considered "defective" by Amazon's standards.

Amazon calculates this metric in terms of the number of orders with a defect divided by the number of orders received during the time period of interest. This metric holds significant weight with Amazon because it directly correlates to the ability of a seller to provide a positive customer service experience.

WHAT IS LATE SHIPMENT RATE?
Usually when a customer places an order, they make a request for some type of shipping method. Each shipping method typically provides an expected shipment date. The seller is then informed of the duration it will take for him or her to deliver the product. If the seller fails to meet the expected shipment date due to nonavailability of inventory or due to shipper's delay, these orders fall under the late shipment category.

The late shipment rate is calculated according to the number of seller-fulfilled orders with a ship confirmation that is completed after the expected ship date divided by the number of seller-fulfilled orders processed during the same period of time. Amazon typically requires that all sellers maintain a late shipment rate below 4 percent.

WHAT IS CANCELLATION RATE?

Amazon creates a listing of the items on its website according to the description of the inventory provided by the items' corresponding seller. The seller must maintain accurate records of its inventory and must fill orders accordingly. However, in some cases an order cannot be fulfilled, and must be cancelled by the seller due to their improper inventory management.

Typically, the cancellation rate is calculated by the number of orders canceled by the seller prior to ship-confirmation divided by the number of orders processed during the same time of interest. When computing this metric, Amazon considers all order cancellation initiated by the seller for any reason.

Three

MAP Pricing

A Minimum Advertised Price (MAP) is an agreement between a manu-facturer and a reseller. Manufacturers inform their distributers and retailers of a set price and that retailer may not sell below that set price. However, there are no restrictions on how much higher the seller may set a price. This is done to protect the manufacturer from the product being sold at a lower cost than the brand wants. It protects profit margins and hurts retailers when consumers do not want to value the product as high as the manufacturer would like the product valued.

In a United States Supreme Court case, *Leegin Creative Leather Prods. v. PSKS*, the court found that, "The manufacturer instituted a retail pricing and promotion policy, refusing to sell to retailers that discounted its goods below suggested prices. The United States Supreme Court decided to overrule the per se rule and determined that vertical price restraints were to be judged according to the rule of reason. The rule of reason was the appropriate standard to judge vertical price restraints and vertical minimum resale price maintenance agreements because (1) pro-competitive justifications existed for a manufacturer's use of resale price maintenance, (2) the primary purpose of the antitrust laws was to protect inter-brand competition, (3) administrative advantages were not sufficient in themselves to justify the creation of per se rules, and (4) stare decisis did not compel the Court's continued adherence to the per se rule[1]."

CJ's Legalese to English

In the Legion case, the United States Supreme Court stated that MAP agreements were not enforceable except against the people and companies that signed them. There is an exception: if the product is something that is really important and the courts think that price levels should be maintained to promote important innovation, then it might enforce the MAP pricing against people who did not sign it. For example, if a manufacturer has a life saving device, then the court might not let people undercut prices by obtaining grey market goods. However, if you are selling a particular brand of shoes, make up or running shirts, then there is no reason to hold anyone to a contract they never signed.

MAP agreements have been the source of a significant amount of baseless complaints against Amazon sellers. In fact, Amazon states in its e-mails to companies that assert MAP complaints that it does not enforce these types of agreements.

---

1 Leegin Creative Leather Prods. v. PSKS, Inc., 551 U.S. 877 (June 28, 2007).

So, what do manufacturers and brands do instead: they assert base-less intellectual property right complaints. These are also called "right owner's" complaints.

Many manufacturers and brand managers seem to be unaware of the extent of damage that they cause to Amazon sellers when they as-sert baseless complaints. Those who do not sell on Amazon seem to be unaware of how poorly Amazon treats their sellers. Most manufactur-ers, their brand managers, and even their lawyers seem to be unaware that when they assert baseless intellectual property right complaints, they put single moms, veterans, and small and large businesses out of business.

When Amazon suspends a seller's account based upon a baseless intellectual property complaint, Amazon requires sellers to contact the complainant and try to persuade the complainant to withdraw their com-plaint. When handling these situations, we typically approach a manufac-turer, brand manager, or lawyer in three steps:

1. We send an e-mail explaining the magnitude of their allegation and explain why their complaint is baseless under US law. We politely ask the brand to withdraw their baseless complaint. We explain to the seller that the Amazon seller was not infringing on any intellectual property rights. We provide a point-by-point anal-ysis of intellectual property law that explains that there was never any: trademark, patent, trade dress, or copyright violation. Most of the time, we are able to negotiate with the brand and obtain withdrawals of baseless complaints.

2. When brand refuses to withdraw their baseless complaint, or ignores our first letter, we then send a second letter. This time, we explain the legal ramifications of their refusal to withdraw their baseless complaint. The brand is politely (maybe not quite

as friendly as the first letter but still politely) informed that as the party making a claim, they must show first and foremost that they have obtained valid trademark, trade dress, copyright, or patent protected under the USPTO. That when push comes to shove, the brand must establish certain elements in order to be successful in a claim against an Amazon seller. For example, if the complaining party alleged trade-dress infringement, they must show that the Amazon seller caused a likelihood of customer confusion.

If a brand accuses a seller of selling counterfeit products, and the product is genuine but being obtained through holes in the brand's distribution system, then there is no counterfeiting. Once a complaining party is made aware of their mistake and how they fail to meet the legal elements to have a claim against a seller, they will usually remove their complaint.

3. There are stubborn brands that ignore our letters. They do not care that their complaint is faulty; they do not care that they are putting someone out of business. What do they care about? Making money by thwarting competition. Our third letter to brands that refuse to remove their complaints is to inform them that things they do can have serious implications on them: let them know that their heads are on the chopping block. For example, if the brand is selling on Amazon, and we can show that their complaint is merely stopping competition and raising prices for Amazon's consumers, then their Amazon account is at risk. Amazon sellers are not supposed to assert or maintain bogus complaints. Amazon protects their customers against all, including brand managers. Also, in our third attempt to persuade the brand to withdraw their baseless complaint, we explain how the brand may be liable for our seller's damages. Brand managers are often unaware that they are subjecting their brand to potential litigation and really bad press if they refuse to withdraw their baseless complaint.

More and more manufacturers are filing complaints they know are baseless, just to kick off members who violate MAP agreements. There is a hole in their distribution, and while they need third-party sellers, they are still willing to kick them off if they do not follow the MAP. We have seen eyeglass companies go after third-party sellers regardless of these businessmen and women selling authentic items. Amazon is a tricky business to navigate, but fortunately, most manufacturers who file fake complaints are willing to remove them once they are aware of their offense.

Amazon themselves have taken a step to combat this issue. They have created a forum that sellers and customers may access.

Customer Discussions
Where's the Price? forum

Showing 1-25 of 222 discussions

Discussion	Replies	Latest Post
Announcement Welcome to the "Where's the Price?" forum!	804 0 new	May 26, 2017
Amazon raises prices even when something is in your cart!	190	2 days ago
Amazon is no longer a serious place to buy.	4	17 days ago
Manufacturer Minimum Advertised Price (MAP)	341 20 new	Jun 16, 2017
Hiding the price loses my business	8	Jun 3, 2017
This is just plain ...... WRONG!	1	Jun 1, 2017
Hidden prices are a FRUSTRATION	29	May 22, 2017
How do you remove a product from cart????	0	Apr 28, 2017
price hidden: una estupidez!!!! no compro!!!!	9	Apr 26, 2017
Hidden exact price	8	Apr 22, 2017
ink cartridges no. 62	0	Apr 16, 2017
hiding price and who is selling item.	0	Mar 24, 2017
No Price, No Purchase	12	Mar 16, 2017
Price jumps after purchase	5	Feb 19, 2017
that is a big stupid idea of new Manager/VP/director	0	Jan 10, 2017

The forum allows customers and sellers to interact with one another to discover the pricing of certain items. The forum clearly states the disagreement with MAPs mentioning, "However, some manufacturers have imposed "Minimum Advertised Price" (MAP) policies that restrict how retail prices may be displayed if they are lower than the manufacturer's MAP price. (Retailers still have the legal right to set their own retail price independently.)"[2]

If you decide to sign a MAP agreement, it is important to know that you may be falsely accused of intellectual property violations on Amazon. Fortunately, there is hope. Make sure you have invoices and documents to first demonstrate that you are in the business of selling authentic items. Your next step would be to hire an experienced attorney to handle the legal issues that arise. Do not try to handle your legal issues alone. Even if you did not break the law, you are still accused of breaking the law, and an attorney will know how to demonstrate to a manufacturer that you have not violated any rights. Once a complaint is removed, you will need to show in your plan of action that the complaint was removed, the party has admitted their mistake, and then you will need to prove that you only sell authentic items.

---

2 Amazon.com, Forum Moderator.

Four

Restricted Categories

Amazon does not allow all sellers to sell all items or in all categories. Sellers are obligated under their contract with Amazon[3] to remain up to date on the restricted lists of products and list of categories that

---

3 Amazon sellers generally do not know that the Terms of Service and their Participation Agreement are not the contract they have with Amazon. If you click through the definitions sections, you will be lead to the Business Services Agreement ("BSA") that is the contract that Amazon sellers have with Amazon. Amazon sellers can easily find the agreement by Googling "Amazon Business Services Agreement."

require approval before selling. Sellers are often suspended for assuming that the products sold by other sellers are not restricted or do not require approval. Just because you see another seller doing it, does not mean they are not violating Amazon's policies. That simply means they were not caught yet or they have Amazon's approval.

Many products require approval from Amazon first. As of July 2017, the following products are listed on Amazon as requiring approval:

- Automotive and power sports
- Beauty
- Clothing and Accessories
- Collectible Books
- Collectible Coins
- Entertainment Collectibles
- Fine Art
- Gift Cards
- Grocery and Gourmet Foods
- Health and Personal Care
- Independent Design
- Jewelry
- Luggage and Travel Accessories
- Major Appliances
- Services
- Sexual Wellness
- Shoes, Handbags, and Sunglasses
- Sports Collectibles
- Textbook Rentals
- Video, DVD, and Blu-ray
- Watches
- Wine[4]

---

4 *Categories and Products Requiring Approval*, Amazon.com Help: Categories and Products Requiring Approval, https://www.amazon.com/gp/help/customer/display.html/?nodeId=14113001 (last visited Aug. 10, 2017).

Additionally, the following products according to Amazon are prohibited from FBA:

- Any product that cannot be lawfully sold and distributed in all US jurisdictions
- Alcoholic beverages (including nonalcoholic beer)
- Sky lanterns or floating lanterns
- Vehicle tires
- Gift cards, gift certificates, and other stored value instruments
- Products with unauthorized marketing materials (e.g., pamphlets, price tags, or other non-Amazon stickers). Note: Amazon will not accept pre-priced labels or products
- Products that are larger than 144 inches by 96 inches by 96 inches or weigh more than 150 pounds
- Products that require prep that have not been prepped according to FBA Packaging and Prep Requirements
- Loose packaged batteries
- Damaged or defective units. Note: Used condition products may have damage as long as the product is labeled with the appropriate condition
- Products with labels that were not properly registered with Amazon before shipment or that do not match the product that was registered
- Products that do not comply with any agreement between Amazon and the seller
- Products that have been illegally replicated, reproduced, or manufactured. We reserve the rights to destroy and to deny removal requests for any inventory identified as counterfeit.
- Products that Amazon otherwise determines are unsuitable.[5]

Unfortunately, the last "catch all" restriction can get sellers into trouble. Remember, you must be proactive in your business, double check that

---

5 *FBA Prohibited Products*, Amazon.com Help: FBA Prohibited Products, https://www.amazon.com/gp/help/customer/display.html?nodeId=201790610 (last visited Aug. 10, 2017).

what you are selling is approved and in accordance with Amazon's policies. Prevention is the best method. Here, it is not best to "do first, ask for forgiveness later."

Amazon restricts the sale of anything illegal, unsafe, or products requiring a prescription. If Amazon catches you selling anything that is restricted, it is best to admit your mistake and move forward. Your POA should not blame anyone else, and should especially not blame Amazon. Don't bite that hand the feeds you.

STEP ONE:

Dear Product Compliance Team,

I am a principal of (Your Store), and we are writing this to appeal our suspension due to mistakenly listing a restricted product for sale on the Amazon platform.

ASIN:

Title:

THE ROOT CAUSE OF THE ISSUE

- We failed to review Amazon's policies and restricted-item lists before listing our products. We made an honest mistake and listed a restricted product.
- We incorrectly assumed that the item was not restricted because this ASIN already existed on Amazon and other sellers are active on the listing.

In this situation, a seller was kicked off even though other sellers were also selling the same restricted product. Unfortunately, the seller assumed that the product was not restricted because they knew the product was being sold on Amazon. Amazon has a system in place to detect those selling restricted products, and if you are detected, you are guilty, even if everyone else is doing it. Your next section in your Plan of Action should contain your Immediate Corrective Actions. The Immediate Corrective Actions section should include what you did to make the customer happy as soon as you learned of an issue and also what you immediately did to prevent more complaints.

STEP TWO:

We understand the responsibility for policy compliance lies with us. As such, we have taken the following actions to correct this issue and ensure it never reoccurs:

IMMEDIATE CORRECTIVE ACTIONS

- We have removed all the products at issue from our inventory and are never going to sell this product, or any similar product, on Amazon in the future (our listings are closed/deleted for the ASIN).
- We analyzed all our listings against restricted-item lists to ensure full compliance.
- We now only sell quality items that are in compliance with Amazon's policies.

We analyzed our listings against all of Amazon's policies to eliminate any misleading elements, policy violations, and to otherwise to improve our policies for preventing future issues on Amazon.

For example, Amazon sellers should always refund the customer and consider removing the listing or their inventory until they have a chance to perform a thorough review of the product. Remember to incorporate the leadership principles that we discussed earlier; this is where you will incorporate those key words.

Your final step in your plan of action is showing exactly how you are changing your business to prevent the same or similar issues from occurring again in the future. If you can phrase the systemic changes in the past tense, it is better to have made the changes rather than make promises of change. You should show not only that you would review Amazon's policies on a frequent basis to ensure you do not list a restricted product again but also show *how* you will do so.

STEP THREE:

SYSTEMIC CHANGES TO OUR BUSINESS TO PREVENT SIMILAR ISSUES

- We dedicated a team member to specialize in policy and compliance specifically for the Amazon platform.
- We do not sell any restricted items on the Amazon platform. Before listing any new items, we analyze all new items against Amazon's policies to ensure we do not list any restricted products.
- Despite our setbacks, we now check reports, metrics, notifications, e-mails, feedback, and reviews twice daily to identify and prevent issues. A designated employee now immediately responds to all customer concerns and addresses all performance notifications promptly and thoroughly, including those regarding product, listing, and category restrictions.

Your conclusion should state that you take full responsibility, and that you have taken all actions to correct and prevent this issue from occurring in the future in a timely fashion.

Five

Related or Multiple Accounts

Many sellers are suspended because they either maintain or are accused of maintaining "related" or multiple accounts.

Amazon imposes on sellers one of the worst business practices that exists: a lack of diversification. Basic business common sense is that you should not have all of your eggs in one basket. You should not have all of your money or all of your income from one source or a single product. If you do, you are always at a significant risk of losing your income.

In fact, Amazon's insistence that its' sellers only have one account and put all their apples in one basket flies in the face of Amazon's incredible and never-ending diversification. There are likely multiple or dozens of sellers selling the same product as you sell on Amazon. Amazon is not reliant on you for their business of providing its customers with every imaginable product on earth.

While Amazon imposes a lack of diversity on you, the company has diversified itself and is not reliant on any one mechanism for any of the following:

- Shipping—Amazon uses the United State Postal Office, UPS, its own trucks, planes, and temporary drivers and delivery personnel that it pays by the hour as needed. As far as the author is aware, Amazon is either the only or one of few companies that was able to get the USPS to negotiate rates after Amazon slowed down its reliance on the USPS during a dispute over rates.
- Sellers—Not only does Amazon have sellers lined up behind you if you do not want to sell on its platform, get suspended, or kicked off, but Amazon is believed to use the data from your sales to choose what products it is going to sell itself and compete against you.
- Specific Products:
  - Merchandise By Amazon
    - Amazon can print its own novelty T-shirts, hats, and so on. At a great biannual Amazon sellers' event called SCOE, it was described as Amazon having purchased hundreds of half-million dollar machines to print its own T-shirts, and so on. Novelty T-shirt sellers should diversify ASAP.

- Amazon has created its own line of fashion.
- Electronics
  - Amazon purchases and sells electronics on its own that compete directly with your products.
- Home Consumables
  - In addition to many products, have you seen Amazon's Dash Buttons? If you are selling consumables like laundry detergent, toilet paper, paper towels, deodorant, and many other lines of products, think about whether or not you want to compete directly against Amazon or look for other products.

BUSINESS DECISION: ACCOUNT DIVERSIFICATION VERSUS RISK OF SUSPENSION OR BAN FROM AMAZON

If you are thinking about opening a second account to sell on Amazon without Amazon's permission, you should evaluate the risk versus the reward just like any other business decision.

The risk of opening up a second, third, or fifteenth Amazon account without Amazon's permission is that if you get caught, Amazon will suspend both or all of your accounts. You can be banned from the platform. On the other hand, if you only maintain one account and that account gets suspended or closed, your entire Amazon business stops or ends.

What is less risky for you? Which provides a better risk versus reward analysis?

HOW AMAZON CATCHES PEOPLE/COMPANIES WITH MULTIPLE OR RELATED ACCOUNTS

First, the following information was compiled through attending Amazon trade shows, like Global Sources' Amazon Summit in Hong Kong, The Sellers' Conference for Online Entrepreneurs in Seattle and Philadelphia, Midwest e-Com in Minneapolis, Prosper in Las Vegas,

Compass in Chicago, Online Sellers UK, Brighton SEO, Linnworks in the UK, Ed Rosenberg's Facebook group and his events in New York, CPC Strategies' awesome online webinars, books and articles, and speaking with countless sellers and former Amazonians from around the world. None of the information below can be attributed to any specific source.

Through innumerable hours and miles on planes, trains, and cars, it seems clear that Amazon can link multiple accounts to each other through some or all of the following:

- Name(s) of account holders including maiden names and married names
- Addresses of account holders
- Bank account information
- Identical or very similar inventory
- Ownership of domain names and websites
- Hosting of domains and websites
- IP addresses used to log onto accounts
- Computers used to log onto accounts
- Smart phones used to log onto accounts
- Names of business or storefronts
- Names of brick-and-mortar stores where sellers may also sell products
- Spreadsheets used to upload inventory
- Type of products sold
- UK Accounts and Foreign Accounts
    - Utility bills submitted for account verifications
    - Foreign company identification numbers (Chinese sellers need to be especially careful when they receive updated business certificates from the Chinese government and make conscious decisions what, if anything, to submit to Amazon.co.uk)

- Responses to verification requests for information and documents
- Use of outside companies to help set up your Amazon account (generally not needed, and this might create additional risks for you.)
- Former significant others, especially partners with whom you shared an address, and after you separate, each one of you open or maintain Amazon sellers' accounts
- Spouses with separate businesses on Amazon
- Parents and children with separate businesses on Amazon
- Shared warehouses
- Shared office space

Amazon has detected accounts by sending out e-mails to sellers asking if they have multiple accounts. This is a copy of an e-mail some sellers received:

"Dear Seller,

As we continue to ensure our marketplace is safe and trustworthy for both buyers and sellers, we would like your help. Amazon prohibits the use or maintenance of more than one seller account. We understand that in certain circumstances you may need to use multiple accounts or associate one or more accounts to your seller account. In an effort to better understand the business requirements that you may have for multiple or related accounts, we request you to list these accounts in Seller Central along with the reason for relating them to your seller account.

Simply click or copy and paste the link below into your web browser to access your account within Seller Central and provide any and all e-mail addresses and reasons for their use—it's that easy.

https://sellercentral.amazon.com/related-accounts

For more information, see the following Help page:
https://sellercentral.amazon.com/gp/help/202146190

Regards,
Amazon Services"

This is one way that Amazon is able to "catch" those who are maintaining multiple accounts. Unfortunately, those who do not have multiple accounts have also received this letter and have been suspended under false accusations of having more than one Amazon account.

HOW TO MAINTAIN MULTIPLE ACCOUNTS

If you have multiple Amazon accounts or have made the decision to open multiple accounts, you need to be very careful to avoid detection by Amazon. This means that you must be flawless in your operation and flawless in maintaining the separate accounts.

With the list above, you have a basic, but *not a complete* list of issues that you must consistently...perfectly, maintain.

Simple Advice: You must never, not even once, sign onto both of your accounts from the same computer. Even with different computers, you must never sign onto more than one account from one IP address. Do not use your smart phone on more than one account. I suggest that you never log onto any accounts from home because you might make an error or, most likely, someone else in your home who shops on Amazon could make an error and log onto different accounts from the same computer or IP address.

You may want to treat each account like its own separate brick-and-mortar business. Each account can have its own physical address where the staff for that account work and the other accounts are located elsewhere.

You may choose to forego traditional economies of scale. You might be well advised not to share resources among your multiple accounts because the short-term savings of using the same bookkeeper may result in that bookkeeper making a mistake and your accounts being linked and shut down. You might want to forego the short-term savings for the long-term diversification and profitability of maintaining multiple accounts.

MULTIPLE ACCOUNT SUSPENSION POA

If you are caught violating Amazon's multiple accounts policy, then you will need to create a comprehensive Plan of Action that demonstrates to Amazon that this was a mistake and that it will never happen again. If you had made an honest mistake, mention that. Perhaps you and your spouse maintain separate businesses, but share the same IP address. Whatever your reason, you will need to show to Amazon that the mistake was yours and that you have corrected that mistake.

STEP ONE:

Dear Product Compliance Team,

I am a principal of (Your Store), and we are writing this to appeal our suspension due to mistakenly maintaining multiple accounts.

THE CAUSE OF THIS ISSUE:

- My spouse and myself maintain two completely separate business accounts, however, we do share the same IP address.

Once you have discovered why your account was linked to another, you must demonstrate exactly how you corrected the issue to Amazon. Simply stating that your spouse has a different business and Amazon is incorrect to label them multiple accounts will not work. You need to move one business to a different IP address; treat it like an entirely separate business.

Your next step within your Plan of Action is to show how this will never happen again. Sometimes, the issues are not as easy to resolve. You will need to incorporate the business practices to show Amazon that this issue will not reoccur. Showing proof of changed documentation is one step that will demonstrate that you took the issue seriously.

STEP TWO:
We understand the responsibility for policy compliance lies with us. As such, we have taken the following actions to correct this issue and ensure it never reoccurs:

CORRECTIVE ACTIONS:

- Moved one business to a different IP address in a timely fashion
- Updated all information so that each store has its own IP address, inventory, business information, addresses, bank information, and manufacturer

STEP THREE:

PREVENTATIVE MEASURES

- We made key inputs into our separate businesses and have each dedicated a team member to specialize in policy and compliance specifically for the Amazon platform.
- Please see attached proof of all changed documentation to demonstrate these are two entirely separate businesses.

- Hired extra staff to routinely check that all personal and business information does not overlap between the two separate businesses.

Your conclusion should mention that despite these setbacks, you have made the appropriate changes and will only continue to sell quality products while abiding by Amazon's policies.

WHAT IF YOU ARE FALSELY ACCUSED OF HAVING MULTIPLE OR "RELATED" ACCOUNTS?

If you are falsely accused of having related accounts, you have a significant problem. It seems that when Amazon accuses a seller of having related accounts, Amazon is convinced that it is correct. Convincing Amazon's staff that Amazon made an error is difficult.

The first step in addressing the suspension of your account based upon a false allegation of having related accounts is to do a thorough investigation of your business—in Amazon language, a "deep dive."

A seller suspended after being falsely accused should examine at least all of the following to try and find a link between your business' account and any other Amazon account:

- Employees:
    - Do any of your employees have their own sellers' accounts?
    - Are any of your sellers signing into your business' account from their homes?
    - Are any employees using their phones to sign into your business account?
    - Are any of your employees signing into their personal buying accounts from your office? Is your staff shopping on Amazon from work?
- You / The Business Owner:

- Are you signing in from home where someone else, a spouse for example, also has a separate Amazon account?
- Are you signing in from your phone from various locations?
- Do you have both a business account and a personal buying account?
- Product Line:
  - Did you upload your inventory from a spreadsheet that was created by a vendor or distributor? If you did, that spreadsheet may have been used countless times and may have triggered a Related Accounts problem.
  - Does your inventory too closely match other stores? If you are working closely with other Amazon sellers, distributors or manufacturers, your inventory may trigger a Related Accounts problem;
- Location
  - If you are in an urban environment, like Brooklyn, New York or Shenzhen, China, there are thousands of Amazon sellers in your locale. You may have dozens or more Amazon sellers in your building or, in China, e-commerce industrial park.
  - If you are sharing space of shipping your products from shared warehouses, this may trigger a Related Accounts issue.

PLANS OF ACTION WHEN FALSELY ACCUSED OF HAVING RELATED ACCOUNTS

When you are falsely accused of maintaining Related Accounts, we suggest that you follow the same format as most Plans of Action: Root Causes of the Accusation; Immediate Corrective Actions; and Long-Term Systemic Changes to Your Business.

For your Root Causes, you may want to discuss the results of your "deep dive" investigation into your staff, inventory warehouses, and so on. You may want to discuss that you identified two or more employees who have their own sellers' accounts or who were using company computers or their phones through your Wi-Fi to shop.

Your Immediate Corrective Actions should include that you prohibited employees from selling on Amazon outside of their positions with your company; that you coached your staff on the importance to Amazon that its sellers only maintain one (1) account; and that you stopped what you were able to identify.

Long-term changes to your business might include adding to your interview process, investigation and training of employees that they may not have other Amazon accounts and cannot access their personal accounts from work.

Six

Intellectual Property Complaints & Suspensions also called "Rights Owner" Complaints & Suspensions

As an Amazon seller, you should be aware of the Intellectual Property (IP) issues that regularly arise when selling on Amazon.

First, the basics of Intellectual Property. Intellectual Property for Amazon sellers involves:

- Copyright Claims
- Allegations of Trademark infringement
- Trade Dress accusations
- Claims of Patent violations.

WHAT IS A COPYRIGHT?

Copyright law, as it comes into play for Amazon sellers, generally deals with the use of someone else's images or verbiage. There are three traditional types of copyright infringement: direct, contributory, and vicarious.

1. **Direct** copyright infringement requires the "plaintiff" to show that he or she owns the copyright and that the defendant personally violated one of the plaintiff's rights enumerated in the Copyright Act. The catch is that a third party who does not directly infringe could be held liable for secondary infringement."[6]

2. **Contributory** copyright infringement means "an actor had knowledge of the activity and induces, causes, or materially contributes to the infringing conduct of another."[7]

3. **Vicarious** liability for copyright infringement takes place when the accused "enjoys a direct financial benefit from another's [directly] infringing activity and has the right and ability to supervise the infringing activity," but declines to stop or limit it[8]. "It is predominantly secondary infringement that concerns Amazon sellers because they are often accused of hosting the product listings that are allegedly infringing a copyright."[9]

---

6 Robert Segall, E-Commerce, Amazon, and the DMCA: Fighting Copyright Bullying in the Modern E-Commerce Context.

7 *Id.*

8 Ellison v. Robertson, 357 F.3d 1072, 1076 (9th Cir. 2004).

9 Segall, *Supra* note 6.

Congress enacted Title II of the Digital Millennium Copyright Act (DMCA) in 1998.[10] The DMCA was created, according to congress, to address "the controversial questions of copyright liability in the online world.[11]"

The DMCA offers safe harbor provisions to provide protections for Internet service providers who may have been held to be liable for copyright infringement[12]. DMCA §512(c) states that "when a service provider receives an official notice of an infringement allegation from a copyright owner, they are required to 'expeditiously remove or disable access to the infringing material[13].'" The four safe harbors provided by Congress, in the text of Section 512, are:

(a) Transitory digital network communications
(b) System caching
(c) Information residing on systems or networks at the direction of users
(d) Information location tools[14].

Additionally, there is the "The Online Copyright Infringement Liability Limitation Act ("OCILLA"). This law protects Internet service providers ('ISPs' or 'service providers') from liability for monetary relief for direct, vicarious, and contributory infringement and, often, from injunction where infringing or allegedly infringing materials are carried on the system without the knowledge and involvement of the service provider[15]." Amazon, along with other e-commerce websites like eBay or Alibaba, are considered ISPs.

---

10 Digital Millennium Copyright Act of 1998, 17 U.S.C. § 512 (2016).

11 *See* Ellison v. Robertson, *Supra* note 8.

12 Weinstein, *supra* note 3.

13 17 U.S.C.S. § 512.

14 *Id.*

15 Debra Weinstein, *Note, Defining Expeditious: Uncharted Territory of The DMCA Safe Harbor Provision: A Survey of What We Know and Do Not Know About the Expeditiousness of Service Provider Responses to Takedown Notifications*, 26 Cardozo Arts & Ent L.J. 589 (2008).

WHAT IS A TRADEMARK?

A trademark is "any word, name, symbol, or design, or any combination thereof, used in commerce to identify and distinguish the goods of one manufacturer or seller from those of another and to indicate the source of the goods[16]."

For example, the Nike swoosh, the M in McDonald's, the way that Gucci writes is Gs, Apple's picture of an apple with a bite taken out of it—these are all valid trademarks. As soon as you see the Apple, you know who made that product and you expect a certain quality. On the other hand, generic words, pictures of items that occur and exist in nature (like drawings of fruits on the packages of supplements) cannot be trademarked.

CJ's Side Note

Items that occur in nature cannot usually be trademarked. This issue arises fir sellers of nutritional supplements where multiple manufacturers employ pictures of drawings of the fruit from the supplement arises. Similarly, the name of naturally occurring substances cannot be trademarked.

The Lanham Act governs trademarks. The federal statute, "governs trademarks, service marks, and unfair competition. The Lanham act outlines the procedure for federally registering trademarks, states when owners of trademarks may be entitled to federal judicial protection against trademark infringement, and sets forth other guidelines and remedies for trademark owners[17]."

---

16 15 U.S.C. § 1127.

17 *See id* § 1051.

Intellectual property issues arise on Amazon primarily when a brand makes a baseless complaint against an Amazon seller that is selling genuine products. There are instances where sellers are selling counterfeit products, but the vast majority of sellers do not sell counterfeit items. Even among Amazon sellers that sell counterfeit products, the sellers do not know that they bought and then resold counterfeit items. Amazon sellers almost always want to sell and try to sell genuine products.

TRADE DRESS

Trade Dress is defined as, "The overall appearance and image in the marketplace of a product or a commercial enterprise. For a product, trade dress typically comprises packaging and labeling. For an enterprise, it typically comprises design and decor. If a trade dress is distinctive and nonfunctional, it may be protected under trademark law[18]."

"The 'trade dress' of a product is essentially its total image and overall appearance. It 'involves the total image of a product and may include features such as size, shape, color or color combinations, texture, graphics, or even particular sales techniques[19].'"

CJ's Legalese to English

Trade Dress basically means how a product or its packaging looks. If a product is using a particular font, color scheme, shape and packaging and you mimic all of the things that make the product look different, you are violating their Trade Dress.

---

18 TRADE DRESS, *Black's Law Dictionary* (10th ed. 2014).
19 Two Pesos, Inc. v. Taco Cabana, Inc., 505 U.S. 763, 765 n.1, 112 S.Ct. 2755, 2755 n.1 (1992).

Amazon does not allow trade-dress infringement on their platform. The Amazon webpage reads, "TRADEMARKS: In addition, graphics, logos, page headers, button icons, scripts, and service names included in or made available through any Amazon Service are trademarks or trade dress of Amazon in the U.S. and other countries.

Amazon's trademarks and trade dress may not be used in connection with any product or service that is not Amazon's, in any manner that is likely to cause confusion among customers, or in any manner that disparages or discredits Amazon. All other trademarks not owned by Amazon that appear in any Amazon Service are the property of their respective owners, who may or may not be affiliated with, connected to, or sponsored by Amazon[20]." Any form of intellectual property infringement against Amazon is a bad idea for sellers. Amazon provides sellers with a list on their customer-service page showing a comprehensive list of all their trademarks.

---

20 *Conditions of Use*, Amazon.com Help: Conditions of Use, https://www.amazon.com/gp/help/customer/display.html/ref=ap_frn_condition_of_use?ie=UTF8&nodeId=508088 (last visited Aug. 10, 2017).

Trademarks and trade-dress rights are published so that all other parties may be aware of the protections. It is a businessman or woman's responsibility when creating a label or logo to first check to see if that design is already protected. Then, it is in the best interest of an Amazon seller to protect his or her logo or label. Many sellers find it difficult to navigate the USPTO, and as a result, they hire an intellectual property attorney to first check for existing marks and then to file for protections.

It is important to protect your brand because the Amazon website has a global audience. Companies do not want competition stealing their designs. Even worse, if you do not receive protections, someone can steal your design, and then file for protections of the design. Unlike patent protections (where you receive protection for twenty years) or copyright protections (where you receive protection for seventy years after the death of the author), trade-dress protections do not have time limits. The trademark protections typically last as long as the mark is used in commerce.[21]

Trade dress often comes into play on Amazon when sellers copy brands' color schemes, packaging, shapes, and so on, when they create their own private-label products.

When a seller is developing his or her private label, he or she should stay away from mimicking, too closely, the overall look or "dress" of another company's products. If an Amazon seller copies the same language of a label, colors, and use similar pictures, but use a different brand name, he or she still might be infringing upon another brand's trade dress. It is a common mistake that sellers make when they believe that since the name is different, their product is OK.

---

21 *How Long Does Patent, Trademark or Copyright Protection Last?*, stopfakes.gov, https://www.stopfakes.gov/article?id=How-Long-Does-Patent-Trademark-or-Copyright-Protection-Last (last visited Aug. 10, 2017).

Unfortunately, baseless trade-dress accusations have resulted in the suspension of many Amazon sellers. Competing sellers have accused others that they have violated a trade dress due to similarities that are not strong enough to constitute trade-dress infringement.

For example, selling the same product and both having "green" bottles, is not a violation of trade dress. We have seen vitamin companies, hair companies, and companies who sell Moroccan oils file complaints against their competition, despite the competition not actually infringing on any trade dress. There is a trend of businesses that believe if they received trade-dress protections, they have a monopoly over every individual portion of their protection. They do not; they have protection of the overall appearance. We have seen companies attempt to knock sellers off for using the same fruit or color as their protected trade dress. That is not enough to constitute infringement. It has to be the overall appearance, not one similarity.

"To receive protection, both of the following must be true:

- The trade dress must be inherently distinctive, unless it has acquired secondary meaning.
- The junior use must cause a likelihood of consumer confusion."[22]

Courts have required that in order for Trade-Dress infringement to exist, there "must be unusual and memorable, conceptually separable from the product, and likely to serve primarily as a designator of origin of the product."[23]

In a lawsuit called *Christian Louboutin v. Yves Saint Laurent Am.*, the United States Court of Appeals for the Second Circuit (the federal court

---

22 *What Is Trade Dress?*, Nolo.com, http://www.nolo.com/legal-encyclopedia/what-trade-dress.html (last visited Aug. 10, 2017).
23 Duraco Products Inc. v. Joy Plastic Enterprises Ltd., 40 F.3d 1431 (3d Cir. 1994).

in New York) held that Christian Louboutin's distinctive red sole design was protectable by trademark (trade dress specifically). This 2012 decision established that while a color alone cannot serve as a trademark (trade dress), a color that has established a secondary meaning might be protected.[24] In this case, the red high-heel sole (red bottom) was decided to be a distinctive symbol of the Louboutin brand. This means that when people see red soles on shoes, they immediately know that the pair of shoes was designed by the Louboutin brand.

Trade dress has been viewed by the courts in two ways: the traditional view and the modern view. The traditional view is "referred only to the manner in which a product was 'dressed up' to go to market with a label, package display card and similar package elements."[25] The modern view has expanded from the traditional view.[26] In *John H. Harland Co. v. Clarke Checks,* the court took a modern approach stating that trade dress should be defined as, "'total image' or 'overall appearance' and 'may include features such as size, shape, color or color combinations, texture, graphics or even certain sales techniques.'"[27]

If you have been accused of trade-dress infringement, it is important to speak to a lawyer. Legal issues should not be addressed by non-lawyer "consultants." Do you think a brand or a brand's lawyer is going to care what a former Amazonian says about intellectual property law issues?

---

24 Christian Louboutin S.A. v. Yves Saint Laurent Am. Holding, Inc., 696 F.3d 206 (2d Cir. N.Y. 2012).

25 Jeffrey Milstein, Inc. v. Greger, Lawlor, Roth, Inc., 58 F.3d 27, 31 (2d Cir. 1992).

26 *Trade Dress: The Forgotten Trademark Right,* Findlaw, http://corporate.findlaw.com/intellectual-property/trade-dress-the-forgotten-trademark-right.html (last visited Aug. 10, 2017).

27 John H. Harland Co. v. Clarke Checks, Inc., 771 F.2d 966, 980 (11th Cir. 1983), cited with approval in Two Pesos, Inc. v. Taco Cabana, Inc., 505 U.S. 763, 112 S.Ct. 2753 (1992).

Only an attorney can assess:

- If the accusation against you has any merit
- Draft a legal opinion letter pointing out the complaint is baseless
- Point out the legal liabilities should the brand refuse to withdraw its complaint
- Stand up to another lawyer with any strength

Amazon sellers should always recall that while Amazon doesn't require the complainant to prove much, ultimately it is the complaining party's burden to prove all elements of any alleged infringement.

They must first demonstrate that they have an item that is inherently distinctive and then they must show that your item causes a likelihood of consumer confusion.

Without proving these legal elements, there is no infringement. When you are accused of infringement, it is important to have a legal professional handle your legal issues to assess if what transpired on the Amazon website was actually intellectual property infringement.

WHAT ARE TRADE SECRETS?

Trade Secrets are "a formula, process, device, or other business information that is kept confidential to maintain an advantage over competitors; information—including a formula, pattern, compilation, program, device, method, technique, or process—that (1) derives independent economic value, actual or potential, from not being generally known or readily ascertainable by others who can obtain economic value from its disclosure or use, and (2) is the subject of reasonable efforts, under the circumstances, to maintain its secrecy."[28]

---

28 Trade Secret, *Black's Law Dictionary* (10th ed. 2014).

WHAT IS A PATENT?

Patents protect ideas such as inventions or technological processes. Amazon.com themselves have been in lawsuits relating to patent infringement based on their own behavior, not just their sellers' behavior. Amazon has also been listed as a defendant in cases "when a third-party Amazon Seller is selling a patented product without the proper license."[29]

Amazon has used the defense in patent-infringement cases that the alleged patent is patent ineligible, (*See Appistry, Inc. v. Amazon.com*, where Amazon successfully showed the patents were invalid).[30] Ineligible means that the patent should never have been issued by the US government.

When dealing with patent issues that arise on Amazon, it is in your best interest to hire an attorney; do not go at it alone. Patent-infringement cases are serious and have the potential to cause greater harm to your livelihood than just a suspension. Lawsuits are costly, and you want someone with legal experience to assist you during the process.

When a party wins a patent-infringement claim, they can recover 100 percent of all the profits made by the sale of a product that infringed on the patent holder's rights. ONE HUNDRED PERCENT—this potential recovery could even lead the largest seller into bankruptcy.

OPERATING ON AMAZON

If you are an Amazon seller using private label or a brand owner, it is likely that you have your own logo. Private labeling is designing a manufactured product for sale under the name of the retailer rather than that of the manufacturer. More and more sellers are using private labeling to secure their business. This process is not specific to Amazon.

---

29 *Id.*

30 Appistry, Inc. v. Amazon.com, Inc., No. 4:13CV2547, 2015 U.S. Dist. LEXIS 24421 (E.D. Mo. Mar. 2, 2015).

When a seller places his or her logo and packaging, he or she is creating a design specific to his or her brand. Once a business owner has turned to private labeling, the next step for many is to trademark their brand.

It is equally, if not more important, to first make sure you do not infringe on any other seller's trademark. If you are caught selling a trademarked item without permission, it could cost you not just your Amazon account but also could result in a lawsuit filed against you. "[O]ften, a manufacturer will sue both the Amazon seller and Amazon.com for trademark infringement; usually in cases where a seller is accused of selling items that are inauthentic, counterfeit, or are sold by an unauthorized reseller."[31] However, Amazon is typically not found to be liable for infringement. You may not be as lucky.

WHAT YOU SHOULD DO IF AN IP COMPLAINT IS MADE AGAINST YOU OR YOUR ACCOUNT

Intellectual property allegations are an entirely different ballgame than your normal complaint. This is not just a customer or seller complaining about a late shipment or defective item. This is a legal issue. You face far more than suspensions if the complaint is legitimate; you face a potential lawsuit.

That is why it is so important to *only receive advice from lawyers*: First and foremost, you should not hire anyone who is not a lawyer to help you with these issues. In addition to my law firm, there are a handful of other lawyers around the United States who have some experience with Amazon sellers. Do not trust your legal issues with a nonlawyer—even if he or she worked at Amazon or had a sellers' account on Amazon. No one without a license to practice law in a Federal Court in the United States should give advice about intellectual property issues. In fact, if any nonattorney has taken money from you in exchange for advice about intellectual property

---

31 Amazon Law Library.

issues, he or she likely violated the criminal law in your state and his or her state that prohibits practicing law without a license.

As we stated earlier, *any* allegation of intellectual property infringement will likely result in the suspension of your listing or your entire sellers' account by Amazon. This is because it is Amazon's way of avoiding liability for the infringement. In *Milo & Gabby, LLC v. Amazon.com*, the court held that Amazon could not be held liable when a third party sold infringing goods on the Amazon platform because Amazon itself did not directly offer to sell infringing goods or engage in any other infringing acts.[32] The way Amazon avoids being sued is to kick off sellers at the first sight of an allegation, then leave the seller to prove they did not infringe on any rights.

FOURTH OF JULY 2017. On Monday, July 3rd and then the days after the Fourth of July holiday, July 5th, 6th and 7th, 2017, there were numerous large Amazon sellers who were suddenly suspended after surviving many IP complaints. Smaller sellers often get suspended by one IP complaint. Larger sellers, except for July 3, 5, 6 and 7 in 2017, withstood many. There seemed to be no rhyme or reason for the sudden suspensions. It was as if any large seller who received one more IP complaint immediately before or immediately after the Fourth of July, was at risk of suspension. As quickly as the sudden suspensions appeared…they stopped.

When your listing or account is suspended, you will see in the e-mail from Amazon that it is requiring you to work out the issue with the person or company that filed the complaint. You need to contact the seller or company who has made the allegation. Many companies have taken the necessary precautions and have properly registered their IP. These companies will have systems in place to monitor for infringement, and

---

32 Milo & Gabby, LLC v. Amazon.com, No. C12-1932RSM, 2015 U.S. Dist. LEXIS 149939 (W.D. Wash. Nov. 3, 2015).

sometimes people who are legally selling authentic products get caught in the net. In many cases, the IP rights are valid, but the allegations are totally baseless.

NOTE—In most cases that we have seen, the allegations are base-less—there is no infringement behind most complaints.

Many complaints arise where your account is selling a product that may appear similar to others, but those specific similarities are not sufficient enough to constitute infringement. You will likely need an attorney to demonstrate to the company that your product is unique, original, and not infringing on anyone's IP rights. If the rights owner does not willingly retract its complaint, it is unlikely that Amazon will reinstate your selling privileges for that item.

There are many times where the complaints are baseless. Companies and manufacturers will also file IP complaints on your account if you are selling the same product, just at a lower price. These types of complaints are without merit, frivolous, and an abuse of the Amazon platform's implemented policy.

Many companies mistakenly allege infringement on Amazon Seller accounts. If this happens, you will need to bring to the complaining party's attention that it is their burden to prove there was an actual infringement. For example, for Patent Infringement, there is an "All Elements Rule" that requires each claim limitation to be proven by the plaintiff who is alleging the infringement. If the company alleging the infringement cannot prove that you have met all the requirements to prove infringement, then there is no infringement, plain and simple. Once it has been established that there was no basis for an infringement claim, the complaining party will usually agree to remove the comment. You will need to have the complaining party state to Amazon, in writing, that the issue is resolved and they are willing to withdraw their complaint. A copy of this document should be attached to your thorough plan of action along with invoices, proving your item has not infringed on anyone's IP rights.

WHEN THE INTELLECTUAL PROPERTY COMPLAINT IS WITHDRAWN

When you are able to obtain the withdrawal of an IP complaint that caused your account to be suspended, your suspension may simply be over. Other times, you may need to take one or several steps to get back to the business of selling on Amazon.

Steps:

1. Make sure that Amazon recognizes withdrawal of the complaint and links it to your suspended Amazon account. In order for the withdrawal to be linked to your account, the withdrawal must come from the same e-mail from which the original complaint was asserted. Also, you may want to provide the person withdrawing the complaint with the following language to use in his or her e-mail to Amazon withdrawing his or her complaint: *"Dear Amazon, we (name of brand that made the complaint) hereby withdraw the intellectual property right complaint previously asserted against _____ (the name of your account or storefront), Seller ID _____ (your seller ID)."*
2. Make sure that you are cc'd on the withdrawal e-mail.
3. Draft a very concise POA explaining the issues in a positive manner.
4. Prepare to e-mail Notice-Dispute@Amazon.com to show that the complaint was withdrawn and your account should be reinstated (include the withdrawal e-mail, and if you are not successful, in your second submission include the letter from the lawyer explaining why there was never an IP infringement).

INTELLECTUAL PROPERTY POA

Once the complaining party has removed their complaint against you, you will be able to move forward with your plan of action. However, if the complaint is not removed within the given time frame required to write your POA, you must submit with a portion of your letter stating that you have reached out to the seller.

STEP ONE:

Dear Product Compliance Team,

I am a principal of (Your Store), and we are writing this to appeal our suspension due to Intellectual Property–related complaints.

THE CAUSE OF THIS ISSUE:

- We sell only 100 percent authentic quality items through our Amazon account; however, a rights owner mistakenly filed a complaint on our account, believing our product was a knock off.
- We have reached out to the seller, and they have since acknowledged their mistake and removed their complaint.

Once you have shown why this happened, you will then need to show all the steps that you have taken to correct this issue. This includes a letter from the seller acknowledging the error, proof that the complaint has been removed, and most importantly, proof that your item is being sold legally.

The third step may be frustrating to demonstrate. You did nothing wrong, so how do you show that this issue will never happen again? This is when you will incorporate your business practices. Show Amazon that you have and will continue to follow their policies. You must demonstrate that you have someone reviewing your inventory to show that all items are legitimate and not violating any other rights.

STEP TWO:

We understand the responsibility for policy compliance lies with us. As such, we have taken the following actions to correct this issue and ensure it never reoccurs:

CORRECTIVE ACTIONS:

- Contacted the complaining party immediately to resolve the issue
  - Please see attached correspondence demonstrating that the complaining party mistakenly alleged an IP violation.
- Contacted our supplier / manufacturer to ensure all our items are 100 percent authentic and not in violation of an IP rights
  - Please see attached invoices and letter from the manufacturer.

STEP THREE:

PREVENTATIVE MEASURES

- We dedicated a team member to specialize in policy and compliance specifically for the Amazon platform.
- All inventory is reviewed upon arrival to ensure they match their listings 100 percent.
- We only conduct businesses with manufacturers who can supply documentation to demonstrate that all items are 100 percent authentic and not in violation of any other person's intellectual property rights.

Your conclusion should acknowledge that you respect Amazon's customers and their trust. State that you have made key inputs into your business practice to ensure that you also follow Amazon's "customer obsession" motto.

WHEN THE COMPLAINANT REFUSES TO WITHDRAW HIS OR HER COMPLAINT

When the complainant refuses to withdraw his or her complaint, if you have not yet hired a lawyer with intellectual property experience and Amazon experience, you should do so ASAP.

When we are faced with a brand that refuses to withdraw a baseless complaint, we use to do two things:

1. We draft a POA for the seller to submit to Notice-Dispute@Amazon.com that states that the complaint is baseless and should be ignored.
2. We then attach a copy of our Legal Opinion Letter—the same ones we sent to the brand, as support for your POA.

What the seller does is: he or she shows the Amazon's staff that the complaint is baseless and then backs the position up with the opinion of a lawyer.

Seven

Inauthentic Item
Suspensions

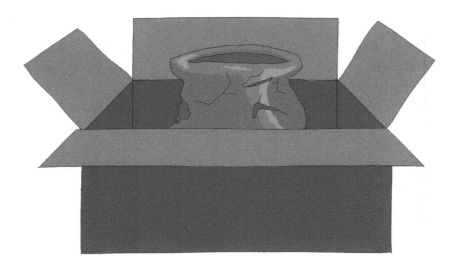

"Inauthentic" does *not* mean fake or counterfeit. Inauthentic means that Amazon wants to know from where you source or obtain your products. "Inauthentic" is an Amazon alteration of what most English-speaking people believe what the word "inauthentic" refers to. If you are selling on Amazon, use their meaning of the word, not your own.

Inauthentic item suspensions are one of the most common suspensions for people and companies selling on Amazon. Sellers who complete a few thousand dollars of sales per month to sellers who does millions of dollars per month suffer the same issues: Amazon sporadically wants to know from where you source your products.

Inauthentic means...*provide copies of your invoices.*

The causes of Amazon issuing a seller an "inauthentic" suspension include all of the following and more:

- Item does not 100 percent match display picture.
- Item does not 100 percent match listing description.
- There is a missing item.
- There is a missing warranty.
- An item is damaged.
- The packaging for an item does not 100 percent match the display picture.
- The packaging for an item does not 100 percent match the listing description.
- The customer was expecting a different product due to misrepresentation on the product detail page.
- Consumer's baseless complaints.

Sometimes, when a seller is faced with an "inauthentic" suspension, the seller determines that it was selling a counterfeit or actually inauthentic item. If this is the case, you should stop selling that item immediately. You should show Amazon that you have detected your mistake, and will never make it again. Part of your plan of action should be showing exactly how you will avoid the problem in the future. This can be achieved by only purchasing from manufacturers that sell authentic items and hiring additional staff to scan your items to assure their authenticity.

Things to look out for: make sure your listings match your item *perfectly*. Your photos should adequately represent the item being sold, as should the product description.

Even the largest sellers, brick-and-mortar businesses, and Amazon itself wind up selling inauthentic items. No retailer wants to sell counterfeit products. But, even with the best intentions and great systems in place, counterfeit items sometimes end up in your inventory.

Gray Market Goods are often the cause of Amazon's "inauthentic" suspensions. Gray Market Goods are usually considered inauthentic, or an IP issue.

Gray Market goods are genuine products that Amazon sellers obtain outside brands' intended distribution channels. Gray Market goods are not fakes or counterfeit. They are the real products. However, Gray Market goods are sold without the brand's consent.

While there seems to have always been a certain number of baseless complaints, during the summer of 2017, the number of complaints by brands skyrocketed. Brands regularly hire attorneys to file Cease and Desist letters. Cease and Desist letters tell a seller that he or she should stop selling the products. Often, a Cease and Desist letter arrives before an actual complaint on Amazon is lodged. They are warning letters. They are shots across the bow.

Amazon sellers need to know a few key points:
- There is nothing illegal in the United States about buying and reselling items without the brand's approval.
- There is a specific law that protects the right in the United States to buy and sell items.
- Even though many complaints are baseless, it is often better for the seller to stop selling the products, even though the seller has every right to continue to sell the product.

INAUTHENTIC ITEM PLAN OF ACTION BROKEN DOWN

Each inauthentic issue is unique; however, here is a basic breakdown of how we approach our plans of actions. First, you will need to introduce who you are, what your business is, what type of suspension you have, and show the issue(s) that caused the complaint(s).

This seller faced inauthentic complaints even though he or she was selling genuine products. However, since the seller's business was not reliant on the product, he or she chose to completely remove the item. There was no good business reason to continue to sell a product that was unimportant financially and created temporary loss of selling privileges.

Each seller's decision and each Plan of Action should be geared to your specific situation and your business practices.

STEP ONE:

Dear Seller Performance,

I am a principal of, (State your Business) and we are writing to appeal our suspension due to inauthentic complaints related to the following items:

ASIN:

Title:

ROOT CAUSE:

We used a search term within our listing titles and keywords to describe the type of product we sell. However, based on our research, we discovered that this term is an unregistered brand name. Even though the term is not a registered trademark, we have decided to remove it from our listings to eliminate any potential confusion.

Your next step in a Plan of Action is to demonstrate your immediate actions when you first learned there was an issue. You should demonstrate all the ways you corrected your issue and tried to assuage the customer. If you do not have access to your account, state what you will do to correct the issue once you have been granted access.

STEP TWO:

CORRECTIVE ACTIONS

- We have taken the following corrective actions:
  - Removed the term from our listings.
  - Ensured that our listings clearly identify our brand name as the product brand.
  - Contacted dissatisfied customers and offered refunds.
  - We also hired an outside firm to perform an analysis of our account to eliminate any potentially misleading elements or terms.
- We conducted a full audit of our inventory and listing details:
  - Inspected all inventory against detailed product information and listing details to ensure they match 100 percent, including type, color, brand, size, and so on.
  - We also inspected each inventory item for quality and condition.
  - We inspected each item to ensure all items are properly packaged, authentic, undamaged, have valid, clear product labels, all seals are intact, and they are exactly as described on Amazon.
  - We inspected all items against detailed product information to ensure 100 percent match.
  - We tested items to ensure they are in proper working order.

Any item showing signs of damage or defect is returned to the manufacturer or manufacturer's facility.

Then, like other Plans of Action, discuss all the new business practices you have implemented to ensure that this issue will not arise again. There are multiple steps you need to take to protect your business, and let Amazon know what they are.

STEP THREE:

LONG-TERM CHANGES TO BUSINESS TO PREVENT FUTURE ISSUES

- Our account management team is now required to review all of our listings against products monthly to reduce and prevent error:
  - Where we identify a potential error, we immediately remove the product until resolved.
  - Where uncertain, we contact Seller Support for guidance.
  - Our legal counsel also performs an analysis for all products and listings on a quarterly basis to eliminate the potential for misleading elements.

Finally, admit responsibility for becoming a better seller. You are selling on Amazon's platform and that is a privilege. While we do not advocate any seller to admit they did anything wrong when they did not do anything wrong, every business person can make changes to improve their business. Take responsibility for making your business better.

CONCLUSION:

"We take full responsibility for the satisfaction of Amazon's customers. My team and I have worked diligently to correct the cause of these complaints and prevent future issues. As such, we respectfully request that Amazon consider our efforts and reinstate our selling privileges. Thank you for working with us to resolve this issue."

Eight

Safety Issue Suspensions

R eceiving a suspension for safety issues, just like intellectual property suspensions, should not be taken lightly. Safety hazards could result in consequences far worse than a suspended account. You do not want to create a product that could harm your customers. That is why if you receive a safety-issues suspension, you must fix the problem immediately.

Many times sellers get kicked off for safety issues and used-sold-as-new complaints at the same time. We have found that when reviewing safety-issue complaints, many of the customers believe the item has been used or opened, and that is what makes the product itself unsafe. Imagine for example, if you purchased a shampoo bottle, but when you received the bottle, the seal was broken. As a customer, you would be fearful that someone had tampered with the product and that the product is not safe to use on your hair. The issue with the bottle is that it is used, and there is a safety risk. These issues occur time and time again, usually due to careless mistakes on behalf of the seller. We have seen many FBA sellers do not have a procedure in place to review items before sending them to customers. The items ship directly from the manufacturer to FBA. As a result, if an item is tampered with during packaging, no one is there to catch the mistake, and the customer files a complaint.

Surprisingly enough, in our experience, safety suspensions have been easier to get reinstated than other suspensions. This is likely because there is a direct issue that can easily be resolved. The "root cause" is usually detectable. Look at your business; was this the result of a failure on your manufacturer? If so, then you will need to show Amazon that you have found a new manufacturer and will never work with the previous company again. There could also be a problem with reviewing your items before they are sent out. Is there someone inspecting all the items to assure they are safe and properly functioning? Whether you are manufacturing in China, Vietnam, India, Thailand, or elsewhere, Amazon sellers should strive to have someone onsite to repeatedly check the quality and also maintain your relationship with the factory.

It is important to implement strict quality standards on the Amazon platform. Simply having many successful sales and happy customers does not make up for the one customer who was injured as a result of your carelessness. When writing your plan of action, it is important to take the initiative.

SAMPLE POA INTRODUCTION:

"We implemented a better system to fully inspect all items for defects and all orders for accuracy before shipping to Amazon's customers. One customer reported that he or she was injured as a direct result of using our product. Because most customers report positive experiences related to using our products, we recognize that this particular customer may have received an item that did not meet our strict quality standards. Because we aim to eliminate all potential for errors, our business administration has implemented the following measures and practices."

What should you look for when you receive a safety-issue complaint? You should review your entire business practice to ensure that it was not many issues within your company that resulted in your suspension. Here is a list of monitoring practices that you may wish to implement:

- Inspect your entire on-hand inventory to ensure compliance with our high condition, safety, accuracy, and quality standards before inventoried, before listed, and before shipped.
- Inspect each item for condition or safety compromises including manufacturing defects, damage, tamper, and improper storage evidence.
- Verify that each item is correctly labeled and packaged exactly as described on its Amazon listing (including size, quantity, etc.).
- Visually verify that all items match the description on their packaging and boxes (i.e., color, size, shape, etc.)
- Verify that each individual order is complete with quality consistent and exactly as described on Amazon.
- Implement a "Three-Stage Manufacturing" quality-control checks to prevent defective items from passing inspection.
- Fully test random items every month to ensure this isolated safety complaint never reoccurs.
  - Verify the product exactly matches the product information and fits or works as intended.

- If a product does not pass the test, then you must deactivate the listing and remove the entire batch from your inventory until potential for defects is ruled out.
- Hold monthly training workshops for all the employees on all of Amazon policies to ensure all the employees are current and in compliance with all quality control and safety-testing procedures.
- Upgrade to high-quality packaging and shipping materials to ensure safe transit to Amazon customers.
  - Make sure a supervisor inspects all orders for accuracy before shipping.
  - To reduce human error, a second employee should inspect orders before the package is sealed to ensure the order is correct and complete.
- If using FBA, upgrade to premium packaging materials to ensure safe transit to customers and Amazon Fulfillment Centers.
  - Review and continue to review our packing and shipping practices against carrier guidelines to ensure safe transit to Amazon fulfillment centers.
  - Fully document and photograph all items before shipping.
- If Your Item Has an Expiration Date:
  - Verify all expiration dates are valid and exceed Amazon's restrictions.
  - Where appropriate, classify products by expiration date:
    - Review all expiration dates monthly.
    - Review "first in—first out" data for accuracy every week to ensure the quality of all orders.
  - Verify the UPC codes, product serial numbers, or other product identifiers against the manufacturer information to ensure that items shipped match the order and listing exactly.
  - Inspect each item to ensure all items are properly packaged, authentic, undamaged, have valid, clear product labels, all safety seals are intact, and they are exactly as described on Amazon.
  - Repeat this inspection process for each item when purchased, before listed, and before shipped.

- Designate an employee to inspect the inventory, invoices, and listings each month to ensure our products are new, complete, undamaged, and exactly match their listings and that quality has been well maintained in storage.
- Any item showing signs of wear, damage, or tamper should be discarded immediately.
- Review and update your listings each month based on product reviews, messages, feedback, and other customer concerns to ensure warnings and details are sufficient to prevent complaints.
- Product Testing—In addition to normal quality-assurance process, you should randomly select samples from each inventory purchase to fully test and discard as follows:
  - Verify the quantity contained matches the label.
  - Verify the product is correctly labeled.
  - Verify that manufacturer quality of the product, its packaging, and physical properties are consistent (color, scent, etc.).
  - Verify the expiration dates are valid and exceed Amazon's restrictions.

Aside from your business practices that will benefit your company, it is also important to make adjustments to your business that will make a difference to Amazon's customer. A customer who sees a negative review regarding safety complaints does not know that you have implemented new procedures, nor do they care. A customer cares about receiving his or her product on time and that the product is not a safety hazard.

HERE ARE SOME BUSINESS PRACTICES TO IMPROVE YOUR OVERALL CUSTOMER SERVICE:

- Follow up with all customers after their confirmed purchase to ensure satisfaction including, detailed product information, our warranty details, and our disclaimer.

- Check all reports, notifications, e-mails, metrics, feedback, and reviews twice daily to identify potential issues.
  - If you receive returns or complaints of 2 percent of orders for the same ASIN, remove that ASIN until the issue is fully resolved.
  - Respond to all customers within twenty-four hours.
  - If you receive an A-to-Z claim, then that customer should receive an immediate refund.
  - If any customer leaves a review of three or less, they should be offered a full refund, and then follow up by requesting for more information regarding his or her complaint.
  - Review transit times and shipping carrier practices to improve customer satisfaction.

If you are both the brand owner and the manufacturer of your product that received safety-issue complaints, then it is your responsibility to take your safety precautions a step further. Yes, you should still examine all of your listings to ensure they are accurate, but there must be more. You are the manufacturer; you are responsible for designing and creating the product that has injured an Amazon customer. Many sellers who are also the manufacturer add legal disclaimers and warranties to create a safer environment for all.

Adding a legal disclaimer against improper use of your product is essential because it may be useful to avoid liability in the future. Make sure your warnings and instructions are clear, easy to understand, and alert the customer so as they do not miss the warning. In your follow-up e-mail to your customers, reiterate the warning to avoid the misuse of your product. We have seen it in the news time and time again about companies failing to warn their customers about the risk of a certain product. Even if the product was misused, they can still be found liable for not warning the customer of the risks involved. First and foremost, protect your business by creating safe and quality products, and secondly by taking the time to warn customers of any risks.

SAFETY ISSUES WITH RETURNED ITEMS

When an item is returned, it is your responsibility to review the item entirely. Returned items should be treated as an item that has not been through your multiple-step system of checking for damage, markings, or any inconsistencies between the used item and the product detail page. The previous customer may have tampered with the product causing enough damage to result in a safety issue. Further, all returned items may not be labeled as new, even if they pass a thorough inspection. All returned items, according to Amazon's policies must be labeled as used.

When an item is returned, properly inspect each item for safety, quality, and condition. It might be in your best interest to designate a separate area within your warehouse for returned products to ensure that you never resell them as new.

FBA Returns. *Opt out, opt out, opt out.* Explanation below.

CJ's Side Note

FBA Returns. If you are an FBA seller and you are allowing returned items to be placed back into your inventory, opt out of this feature. You may lose a few dollars by not reselling items that were returned. However, if you think that Amazon's warehouse staff is carefully reviewing products to make sure that they still appear to be new after another customer receives the product and then returns it, you are kidding yourself. Opt Out. Commingled Inventory. If your FBA account allows your products to be commingled with other sellers' products and other sellers' products with yours, then you are basing the health of your business on any number of sellers who may or may not have your quality control. Opt Out.

SAFETY ISSUES WITH THE MANUFACTURER

If your safety-related issue is due to a mistake on behalf of the manufacturer, then you must state that in your Plan of Action. However, even though it was the manufacturer's error, it was your responsibility to only work with reputable businesses. You plan of action should demonstrate that your root cause of the issue lies within your manufacturer and that you will take new steps to protect consumers. Reiterate to the Amazon team that customers are your number-one priority and you will only provide the best to their customers. The following is a sample plan of action for a seller whose manufacturer caused the safety issue:

STEP ONE:

Dear Seller Performance,

I am a principal of (Your Store), and we are writing to appeal the safety complaints related to the condition of the following products:

ASIN:

Title:

THE ROOT CAUSE OF THE COMPLAINT

- Customers complained about the condition of items they received possibly due to oversights in quality control.
- However, products are sourced directly from the manufacturer. Please see the attached documents proving they are new, safe, and authentic and that we have right to sell these products.

- See attached authorization letter from the manufacturer granting our company the right to sell these items as an authorized distributor within the United States.
- See attached certification proving our manufacturer is authorized to manufacture these types of products.

STEP TWO:

IMMEDIATE CORRECTIVE STEPS WE HAVE TAKEN TO RESOLVE THE ISSUE

- We have removed each of these products from our inventory for thorough inspection to ensure the issues are resolved.
- We have contacted each dissatisfied customer to offer refund and apologies,
  - We have removed each of these products from our inventory until this issue is completely resolved.
  - After each purchase, we provide each customer with complete product information and ensure they have no concerns regarding their purchase.

STEP THREE:

LONG-TERM CHANGES TO OUR BUSINESS TO PREVENT SIMILAR ISSUES
We implemented monthly workshops for all employees to review Amazon guidelines and restrictions to ensure we are up to date on all policies.

- Listing/Labeling/Expiration Date—We inspected our entire inventory and increased the frequency of quality-control inspections.

- Product Testing—In addition to our normal quality-assurance process, we randomly select samples from each inventory purchase to fully test and discard those who do not meet Amazon's standards.
- Sourcing—We requested assurances from our supplier that all products are new, safe, and manufactured and tested under the strictest standards.

Finally, at the end of your plan of action, you should have a short conclusion where you take responsibility. Your conclusion should read something to the effect of: "We accept accountability for the safety and satisfaction of Amazon's customers and aim to provide them with leading product and customer experience as possible. While our business has suffered from this issue, it has given us the opportunity to review our business and become a better seller. We hope our efforts are acceptable enough for Amazon to reinstate our selling privileged for this ASIN. If we can provide any further information about how we have improved our business to prevent further issues, please let me know."

Nine

Used Sold as New Suspensions

A s stated in the previous chapter, safety issues and used-sold-as-new issues typically intertwine on the Amazon platform. If a product is said to be new, but is actually used, a customer may believe it is the result of the product being defective and therefore, unsafe to use. Many times, a used-sold-as-new complaint is filed not because the item is actually used, but instead was damaged en route to the customer. Additionally, an item will be considered used if it was opened or returned. Even if the product was returned and unused, it is not considered new in Amazon's eyes, or the eyes of your customer.

New must mean brand new, never opened before, undamaged pack-aging—new. If your product does not meet these standards, it is not new, and do not label it as such. The following is an excerpt of Amazon's policy regarding condition of items from their webpage:

General Condition Guidelines
The following guidelines apply to all product categories unless other-wise indicated in the Category-Specific Condition Guidelines:

Note: "Refurbished," "Used—Good," and "Used—Acceptable" can be used only where noted as acceptable in the Category-Specific Condition Guidelines.

- *New:* Just like it sounds. A brand-new, unused, unopened item in its original packaging, with all original packaging materials included. Original protective wrapping, if any, is intact. Original manufacturer's warranty, if any, still applies, with warranty details included in the listing comments.
- *Refurbished:* Use *only* if noted in the Category-Specific Condition Guidelines. A refurbished product has been professionally restored to working order. Typically this means that the product has been inspected, cleaned, and repaired to meet manufacturer specifications. The item may or may not be in its original packaging. The manufacturer's or refurbisher's warranty must apply and should be included in the listing comments. Refurbished items are sometimes referred to as "remanufactured."
- *Used—Like New:* An apparently untouched item in perfect condition. Original protective wrapping may be missing, but the original packaging is intact and pristine. There are absolutely no signs of wear on the item or its packaging. Instructions are included. Item is suitable for presenting as a gift.
- *Used—Very Good:* A well-cared-for item that has seen limited use but remains in great condition. The item is complete, unmarked, and undamaged, but may show some limited signs of wear. Item works perfectly.
- *Used—Good:* Use *only* if noted in the Category-Specific Condition Guidelines. The item shows wear from consistent use, but it remains in good condition and works perfectly. It may be marked, have identifying markings on it, or show other signs of previous use.

- *Used—Acceptable:* Use *only* if noted in the Category-Specific Condition Guidelines. The item is fairly worn but continues to work perfectly. Signs of wear can include aesthetic issues such as scratches, dents, and worn corners. The item may have identifying markings on it or show other signs of previous use.[33]

These kinds of suspensions are typically easy to obtain reinstatement. That is because the root cause is easy to detect. First, look into your own business practices. Is there a member of your company reviewing each item before it is shipped? Do you perform routine test-buys to ensure all items are intact? If you source your items from a manufacturer, then it is important to review your relationship with that company. You do not want to face the consequences for a manufacturer's mistake. When sourcing, it is important to follow these business practices:

Sourcing:

- Request assurances from your supplier that all products are new, safe, and manufactured and tested under the strictest standards. (These will be useful when writing your plan of action).
- Only sell new products sourced from authorized manufacturers or distributors and retain all invoices for at least 365 days.
- In addition, when applicable, have your suppliers provide Quality Control Certificates with each inventory purchase.
- Compare each individual item you purchase to detailed manufacturer information to verify that the manufacturer labels, expiration dates, warnings, products information, and product identifiers match across the listing details, products and their packaging invoices, and detailed manufacturer information.
- Verify all items are consistent with Amazon's authenticity, condition, and quality standards to eliminate any potential confusion.

---

33 *Condition Guidelines*, Amazon.com Help: Condition Guidelines, https://www.amazon.com/gp/help/customer/display.html?nodeId=1161242 (last visited Aug. 10, 2017).

- You should have employees catalogue and electronically verify all manufacturer-issued expiration dates, batch codes, and product identifiers.

These are just a few of the practices that could help with your business. However, each business is unique. You should take any additional practices not mentioned to improve the way you operate your business. These are issues you can argue in your POA.

If your used-sold-as-new issue was a direct result of the manufacturer, then you must supply your invoices and authentication records, demonstrating the fault is with the manufacturer, and not your business. After demonstrating to Amazon that you have detected the issue, it is best to not conduct business with that manufacturer. In your Plan of Action, you must show that you have taken preventative measures. The best assurance that this issue will never occur again is to remove the issue entirely; sometimes that means finding a new company to source from.

However, if the issue relies within your business, it can be fixed with a few business practices. All returned items should be organized separately from the rest of your inventory. Pursuant to Amazon's policies, they cannot be sold as new, even if they look new or were never opened. Once your inventory is properly organized, a reviewing process is essential to ensure all items are new, look new, and do not have any damage. You may want to consider having items reviewed upon arrival from the manufacturer, again when packaged, and then one final time before shipping.

Packaging is important! If an item is new, but is not properly packaged, then it could result in a damaged product. While this piece of advice may seem obvious, it should be taken seriously. Amazon has strict standards for packaging as a way to combat the issue of unhappy customers with broken items. On their webpage, they have a list of the appropriate requirements for packaging to ensure customer safety. Poor packaging leads to used-sold-as-new complaints and suspensions.

Packaging requirements

Note: A unit that falls under multiple categories must be prepped according to all applicable prep types. For example, if you are selling bottles of Shampoo and Conditioner as a set, both units will need to meet the Liquid requirements as well as be labeled with a "Sold as Set" sticker so that they are not separated.

Follow these general requirements when shipping Units to Amazon fulfillment centers. Certain products have other specific requirements. Amazon may refuse, return, or repackage any product delivered to an Amazon fulfillment center with inadequate or non-compliant packaging at your expense, and you may also be subject to noncompliance fees.

- Any FNSKU you use on a Unit must be unique and must correspond to one unique product. For example, each assortment type, such as size or color, will have a different FNSKU.
- Each Unit must have an exterior scannable barcode or label (which includes a scannable barcode and the corresponding human-readable numbers) that is easily accessible .
  - For Labeled Inventory, one FNSKU.
  - For qualifying Stickerless, Commingled Inventory, one UPC, ISBN, or EAN.

- Remove or cover scannable barcodes on the outside of a carton that includes multiple Units. Only the individual Units within the carton can have scannable barcodes.

34

Following the proper packaging procedures will help ensure that your quality products are being protected when in transit.

We have addressed many used-sold-as-new complaints. Most of the time, there has been two main causes: improper packaging resulting in a damaged or used-looking product, or a used product accidentally being sent to a customer. The following is a sample plan of action when the root cause is that you accidently sent a used product rather than a new product.

STEP ONE:

Dear Seller Performance,

---

34 *Packaging and Prep Requirements*, Amazon.com Help: Packaging and Prep Requirements, https://www.amazon.com/gp/help/customer/display.html/?nodeId=2 00243250#packaging (last visited Aug. 10, 2017).

I am a principal of (Your Store). I am writing to appeal the removal of the following listing due to a complaint claiming our product "looks used":
ASIN:

Title:

ROOT CAUSE OF THE COMPLAINT:

Amazon received a complaint from a customer indicating that the item he or she received "looks used." We investigated the issue and determined that the customer may have received a damaged or opened product as a result of our use of FBA's "repackage returns" feature. This feature provides Amazon the option to repackage and resell returned items. We believe that a customer may have ordered a new item, yet received an item that appeared to the consumer as being used or returned item.

Your corrective actions should include a refund to the complaining customer, an apology, and a quick adjustment to your business practice. Here, the issue was not having reviewing procedures and not being organized.

STEP TWO:

IMMEDIATE CORRECTIVE MEASURES

- We immediately issued a refund or replacement to any dissatisfied buyers and removed the product from our inventory until this issue is completely resolved.
- We have opted out of FBA's repackaging returns service and otherwise reviewed our shipping and receiving practices.
- We inspected and perfected the remainder of our entire inventory and increased the frequency of quality-control inspections.

You will then need to implement preventative measures to ensure this does not occur again. For example, do you have someone looking over your packaging to make sure it is adequate? Is your packing secure enough so that there is no damage to your packaging or product during delivery? Some sellers have hired staff or worked with other businesses that properly review all inventory before shipment to ensure that all items are not subject to damage. The business procedures stated in the previous chapter should be applied for used-sold-as-new complaints as well.

CJ's Side Note

I have heard people speak about customers being held accountable for abusing the returns policy or other conduct, but I have personally never seen or heard of a buyer being suspended.... neither have any of the attorneys that work for my law firm, lawyers that I work with that represent big brands or any of my staff, family or friends. Even my father who, despite my requests to stop, regularly buys three sizes of all items with the plan of returning two of them, has never received any notice from Amazon about his excessive returns. Dad - please stop hurting sellers.

Your conclusion should accept responsibility for doing better in the future and identify how you are improving your business for Amazon's customers. The policy is simple; the procedures to prevent the issue from occurring again are as well. Invest in your business, invest in preventative measures, and take the steps needed to prevent a future suspension.

STEP THREE:

SYSTEMIC CHANGES TO OUR BUSINESS TO PREVENT SIMILAR ISSUES:

- In addition to our normal quality assurance process, we random-ly select samples from each purchase to fully test and discard as follows:

- We implemented monthly workshops for all employees to review Amazon guidelines and restrictions to ensure we are up to date on all policies.
- We check all reports, notifications, e-mails, metrics, feedback, A-to-Z claims, chargeback claims, and reviews twice daily to identify and correct problems before issues escalate.
- We now separate all returned items to a different department to ensure no used product is accidently sold as new.
- We have implemented a reviewing procedure where all items are inspected upon arrival from the manufacturer, during packaging, and again before shipment to ensure every item is properly labeled, undamaged, and 100 percent matching the product's listing.

Ten

Review Manipulation Suspensions

R eview manipulation is when a customer is offered an incentive in exchange for writing a review. It is against Amazon's policies to manipulate reviews because it skews the authenticity of product reviews.

Amazon's number-one concern is maintaining satisfied customers and that cannot happen if the reviews they read are false or manipulated. Even if the review itself is genuine, if it was produced in exchange for something, that review is tainted in Amazon's eyes.

There are businesses where some sellers pay in exchange for positive reviews. This is the most obvious violation. However, there is a lot of gray area in the topic of manipulated reviews. Many sellers who get suspended for this issue are not aware they are in violation of a policy. Having friends write reviews is also a violation of the policy as is sending discounted products in exchange for reviews.

Amazon's Guidelines in regards to feedback is as follows:

PROMOTIONS AND COMMERCIAL SOLICITATIONS

In order to preserve the integrity of Community content, content and activities consisting of advertising, promotion, or solicitation (whether direct or indirect) is not allowed, including:

- Creating, modifying, or posting content regarding your (or your relative's, close friend's, business associate's, or employer's) products or services.
- Creating, modifying, or posting content regarding your competitors' products or services.
- Creating, modifying, or posting content in exchange for compensation of any kind (including free or discounted products, refunds, or reimbursements) or on behalf of anyone else.
- Offering compensation or requesting compensation (including free or discounted products) in exchange for creating, modifying, or posting content.
- Posting advertisements or solicitations, including URLs with referrer tags or affiliate codes.

THE ONLY EXCEPTIONS ARE:

- You may post content requested by Amazon (such as Customer Reviews of products you purchased on Amazon or received through the Vine program, and answers requested through Questions and Answers). In those cases, your content must comply with any additional guidelines specified by Amazon.
- You may post an answer to a question asked through the Questions and Answers feature (but not a question itself) regarding products or services for which you have a financial or close personal connection to the brand, seller, author, or artist, but only if you clearly and conspicuously disclose the connection (e.g., "I represent the brand for this product."). We automatically label some answers from sellers or manufacturers, in which case additional disclosure is not necessary.

    You may post content other than Customer Reviews and Questions and Answers regarding products or services for which you have a financial or close personal connection to the brand, seller, author, or artist, but only if you clearly and conspicuously disclose the connection (e.g., "I was paid for this post."). However, no brand or business may participate in the Community in a way (including by advertising, special offers, or any other "call to action") that diverts Amazon customers to another non-Amazon website, service, application, or channel for the purpose of conducting marketing or sales transactions. Content posted through brand, seller, author, or artist accounts regarding their own products or services does not require additional labeling."[35]

Unfortunately some sellers are having their accounts and listings hijacked, or had their products counterfeited. When this occurs, you should notify Amazon immediately. Sometimes, Amazon does not respond in a timely

---

35 *Community Guidelines*, Amazon.com Help: Profile & Community Guidelines.

manner. If this occurs, do not write or have friends or family write reviews on this seller if they are using your names and listings. To Amazon, it will look as though you are having friends and family write reviews for your product, even though this was a copycat. We have personally seen a seller who had other buyers with the same IP address write legitimate negative reviews and then be suspect to suspension due to feedback manipulation. If Amazon does not respond to your concerns, try to contact their legal team, or hire an experienced attorney to handle the matter. Writing reviews is tricky, and you do not want to have reviews misconstrued and made to believe they were manipulated.

While feedback manipulation is forbidden on the Amazon platform, it is allowed on different platforms. We have seen circumstances where customers purchased products from different e-commerce platforms and mistakenly used Amazon's platform to post their reviews. The following is a sample plan of action for when sellers offer discounts on other platforms and customers mistakenly write reviews on the Amazon platform.

STEP ONE:

Dear Seller Performance,

I am a principal of (Your Store). I am writing to appeal our suspension due to feedback manipulation.

ROOT CAUSE OF THE ISSUE:

1) *We had made the mistake of providing items at a discounted rate in exchange of reviews.* Our customers who purchased our products from us on different e-commerce platforms mistakenly used Amazon's platform to post their reviews.
   - *Even though the reviews are real and related to the products we sell, they were not verified Amazon purchases.*

- Amazon identified these reviews as manipulation.
2) We sent follow-up e-mails to customers who already provided positive seller feedback to request they also write a product review.
   - Customers write positive seller feedback of their own accord.
   - We believe Amazon may identify this as review manipulation, but we are merely following up with customers who are already satisfied.
   - We did not manipulate the customer or the review or the positive seller feedback.
3) We send follow-up e-mails to dissatisfied customers requesting the customer "reply to this e-mail directly" to resolve the issue, so as not to use Amazon's customer service.
   - Since we mistakenly were guiding them around the Amazon customer service team, we believe Amazon may have identified this as manipulation.
   - However, these e-mails were not manipulating the customer for reviews but rather directing them to our store so we could resolve the situation as soon as possible.

After reviewing the community guidelines, we believe we received this notification due to the last point within the Addition Guidelines for Customer Reviews policy. Within this policy, it states "When we find unusually high numbers of reviews for a product posted in a short period of time, we may restrict the number of non-Amazon Verified Purchase reviews on that product." Due to the factors outlined above, we believe this may be the cause of our suspension. We have implemented the following measures to ensure these issues do not reoccur:

Your corrective actions will need to show more than just stating you will not repeat this mistake. You will need to contact anyone you had previously offered the discount to inform them that this discount will discontinue permanently. This policy violation is taken seriously because feedback manipulation taints the customer experience on Amazon. Amazon customers should be able to trust the reviews they read. Make sure Amazon is aware that you also value the customer experience.

STEP TWO:

We have implemented the following Corrective Measures to immediately correct our mistake:

- Retracted our statement offering discounts in exchange for reviews.
- Contacted customers who purchased our products from other e-commerce platforms to instruct them to only write reviews on the e-commerce platform where they purchased the product, providing a link to direct them to the appropriate venue to write a review.
- Terminated our practice by which we send follow-up e-mails to customers who have already provided positive seller feedback for the product they purchased. We only follow up with customers after purchase to ensure they are satisfied with their product and their experience.
- Contacted all customers who received the discount to inform them that the discount deal has been discontinued indefinitely.
- Updated our business practices including updating all members on Amazon's policies to ensure that each member of our business is up to date on the policies.

Finally, you will need to demonstrate just how this issue will never occur in the future. You have acknowledged your mistake and by incorporating business practices that model Amazon's leadership principles, you are taking the correct steps forward into compliance with their policies.

STEP THREE:

PREVENTATIVE MEASURES:

- Reevaluated our entire business practice and implemented the following:
    - Hired additional staff to review Amazon's policies on a routine basis to ensure we are in compliance with all of existing Amazon's policies as well as future policies.
- Conduct weekly reviews of our business practices to ensure that the company is in full compliance with Amazon's policies.
- Informed all members of our business that discounted items in exchange for reviews is against policy and will never exchange anything for a review in the future.
- We reviewed all of Amazon's policies, especially guidelines for customer reviews, and retrained our entire staff to ensure we are in full compliance. We implemented weekly workshops for all employees on updated Amazon policies to ensure our business is always in full compliance in the future.
- We now check all reports, notifications, e-mails, metrics, feedback, A-to-Z claims, chargeback claims, and reviews twice daily to recognize and remove problematic ASINs before issues arise.
- We retrained our customer service team to ensure the following:
    - All customers receive a response within twenty-four-hours.
    - If any customer leaves a review of three or less, they are offered a full refund.
    - All chargeback claims received a full and immediate refund.
    - We follow up after each purchase to provide all customers with complete product information to ensure they have no concerns regarding their purchase.

Eleven

Hacked Accounts

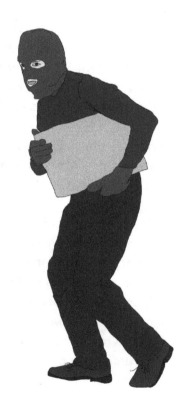

I n the late spring of 2017, Amazon sellers across the globe were faced
with a new beast: hackers. While the issue of having accounts hacked

has existed before, the issue has become far more prevalent. Third-party sellers' banking information was changed. Your distributions were sent to Norway, the United Kingdom, and other countries. "[A]ttackers have changed the bank-deposit information on Amazon accounts of active sellers to steal tens of thousands of dollars from each, according to several sellers and advisers. Attackers also have hacked into the Amazon accounts of sellers who haven't used them recently to post nonexistent merchandise for sale at steep discounts in an attempt to pocket the cash, those people say."[36]

Hackers created listings for products that did not exist. Hackers added inventory the sellers did not maintain. Hackers placed long shipping dates, sometimes up to four weeks so that they may collect money before customers became aware of the scam.[37] Customers on Amazon see highly discounted items, purchase the items, but the item never arrives. The Amazon seller is then held to be accountable until the issue is resolved.

Sometimes, Amazon notifies the seller, and sometimes the seller becomes aware before Amazon. Once Amazon is notified of a hacked account, they typically freeze the account.

The bigger problem? Those whose accounts are stolen are placed in a predicament. They cannot make the necessary changes needed to regain access to their hacked account. They cannot follow Amazon's instructions because they cannot log into their account. Amazon has shut their account down for safety purposes. At this point, contacting Amazon's legal team is necessary. Amazon is willing to work with sellers whose accounts have been hacked so that they may restore their livelihood. Amazon is also working to implement verification procedures to better protect sellers from having their accounts hacked.

---

36 *Amazon.com's Third-Party Sellers Hit by Hackers*, Fox Business (2017), http://www.foxbusiness.com/markets/2017/04/10/amazon-coms-third-party-sellers-hit-by-hackers.html (last visited Aug. 10, 2017).
37 *Id.*

WHY WAS YOUR ACCOUNT HACKED?

Perhaps you went onto a website that installed malware and clicked on a link that steals information. Other ways hackers obtain your information is through e-mails from accounts that you are unfamiliar with. These e-mails can have hacking software if you click on the links. You should beware of anything that requires you to re-log into your account and provide your password that is not the official Amazon website. This means that if you receive an e-mail from an unknown account, you click on the link pro-vided, and that link asked for you to re-log into your account; this may be a hacker. Only provide your account information to the official Amazon website, and never through a secondary website. The hacker will then use your username and password to access your account. It is important to use the two-step verification on the Amazon website so that it is harder for hackers to steal your personal information.

At our law firm, we have had the privilege of working with Amazon's attorneys to resolve hacked account issues and other issues.

IF YOUR ACCOUNT WAS HACKED:

- Notify Amazon immediately (if you discover the hacking before they do).
- Log in from a different computer if possible (to avoid key logging issues that records your key patterns).
- Change your password with the two-step verification process.
- Search your account for any new users who may have been added as a result of your account being hacked. Remove those users.
- Change your settings to "on vacation" until the issue is resolved.
- Cancel and correct all changes to your account, including sales or products.
- Inform
    - Amazon of the hacking;

- all of your business members so as to ensure their personal information is not stolen;
- your bank and ensure all of your information has not been altered. You may need to take this a step further and change your personal bank information to ensure your account is safe; and
- your credit card company or any other personal information that has been provided on your account.

SAMPLE LETTER TO AMAZON

Dear Seller Performance,

I am a principal of (Your Store), and we are writing to address possible unauthorized third-party access to our account.

I received a performance notification stating that my seller account may have been hacked and accessed by an unauthorized party. I was notified that my selling privileges had been suspended to protect my account.

Amazon required we take the following steps toward the reinstatement of our account:

As requested, we have verified the following information is accurate:

- E-mail Address preferences
- Business, shipping and returns, and tax information
- Active and pending promotion codes
- User permissions
- Amazon Storefront
- Listings and condition notes

Further, we have completed the following in order to regain control of our Seller Central account:

- Reset our password with a new, unique password that we do not use for any other account or website.
- We also changed our password for every account that had a similar password (including banking, accounting, and e-mail accounts).
- We also removed any outdated or unnecessary accounts for our Seller Central User Permissions.
- We now also change our password every ninety days as added protection.
- Set up Two-Step Verification in our Advanced Security Settings.
- Sent a confirmation e-mail by clicking the Appeal button next to this message on the Performance Notifications page in Seller Central.

It is important to be proactive with your account security. For now, the two-step security process is something that all Amazon sellers should implement. As for the hacking, the "stranger danger" ideology should apply. Do not trust strangers e-mailing you for your login, and do not trust strange websites asking for your personal information. Another good business practice to implement is to routinely check your bank accounts and your account information. Stay up to date on any changes that seem unusual and notify Amazon if anything occurs. Do not use the same passwords on multiple accounts. For example, if the password to your e-mail account is "Cheesedoodle1234," do not use that same password for your Amazon account.

There has also been an increase in hijacked listings as well. People use other trademarks as their own search terms. When the seller types in the search term, they are not given the true, trademarked item, but rather another seller who hijacked the listing. These sellers can be reported to

Amazon for trademark infringement, and Amazon will likely remove the seller. However, it does not stop there. Some sellers have turned to service provides like Amazon Sellers Lawyer to perform "weekly sweeps." This means that once a week, their trademarked items are checked to ensure others are not infringing on their rights.

CURRENT LAWSUITS THAT COULD SET PRECEDENT FOR AMAZON SELLERS

There have been three lawsuits over the recent years regarding cyber attacks on major online platforms that Amazon sellers should be aware of. Anthem Inc., Yahoo, and Facebook. All were subject to lawsuits after their users had their personal information stolen. In February 2015, Anthem stated that their information technology systems "had been the target of an external cyber attack. The hackers obtained personal information including names, dates of birth, social security numbers, and health-care ID numbers, attorneys said."[38] The company has agreed to a $115 million settlement in the case that had over 78 million people subject to having their personal information exposed. Of those damages, "the company also said $15 million will be allocated to pay actual out-of-pocket costs, up to a set amount, that plaintiffs claim they incurred due to the breach."[39]

Another lawsuit that arose as a result of a cyber attack was *Vail v. Yahoo! Inc.* "On September 22, 2016, Yahoo announced that the account information of 500 million users had been stolen in a hack in late 2014. On December 14, 2016, Yahoo announced that the account information of over one billion users had been stolen in a separate hack in August 2013. [...] Yahoo also indicated that an unspecified number of user accounts were accessed throughout 2015 and 2016 in a third, separate cyber attack involving forged cookies. Yahoo has confirmed that users' real names, e-mail

---

38 *Anthem Agrees to $115 Million Settlement of Data Breach Lawsuit*, Fox Business (2017), http://www.foxbusiness.com/features/2017/06/23/anthem-agrees-to-115-million-settlement-data-breach-lawsuit.html (last visited Aug. 10, 2017).
39 *Id.*

addresses, telephone numbers, encrypted/unencrypted security questions and answers, dates of birth and hashed passwords have all been leaked."[40]

The security breach affected over one billion user accounts. The users filed a class-action lawsuit since not only were they subject to having their personal information taken, but they allege that Yahoo failed to warn the consumers of the breach."[41] The class-action lawsuit asserts Negligence; Breach of express and implied contract and Violation of CA Unfair Competition Law.[42] Further, the "[l]awsuit alleges that the company failed and continues to fail to provide proper protection of its users' private and confidential data. Also, the lawsuit claims that the company failed to provide sufficient and timely notifications regarding the potential cyber-security breaches that could affect its users."[43]

But see also, the Facebook lawsuit has since been dismissed. The lawsuit arose from allegations that Facebook was tracking their user's Internet activity when no longer logged into the website. "U.S. District Judge Edward Davila in San Jose, California said the plaintiffs failed to show they had a reasonable expectation of privacy, or that they suffered any "realistic" economic harm or loss. The plaintiffs claimed that Facebook violated federal and California privacy and wiretapping laws by storing cookies on their browsers that tracked when they visited outside websites containing Facebook "like" buttons. But the judge said the plaintiffs could have taken steps to keep their browsing histories private,

---

40 *Yahoo Class Action—Privacy Breach Class Action Lawsuit,* Yahoo! Privacy Breach Class Action, http://www.yahooprivacybreach.com/ (last visited Aug. 10, 2017).

41 Margaret Cronin Fisk, *Yahoo Failed to Protect Consumers from Hacking, Lawsuit Says,* Bloomberg.com (2016), https://www.bloomberg.com/news/articles/2016-12-15/yahoo-failed-to-protect-consumers-from-hacking-lawsuit-says (last visited Aug. 10, 2017).

42 Anna Aria et al., *Class Action Settlement on Its Way: Vail v. Yahoo! Lawsuit Filed,* Consumer Law Mag. (2017), http://consumerlawmagazine.com/vail-v-yahoo-lawsuit/ (last visited Aug. 10, 2017).

43 *Id.*

and failed to show that Menlo Park, California-based Facebook illegally "intercepted" or eavesdropped on their communications."[44]

What do these lawsuits mean for Amazon sellers? The Facebook lawsuit demonstrates that if an Amazon seller's personal information has been stolen from hackers, it must meet a certain standard for his or her claims to stand. There should be actual economic harm or loss as a result from the hacking. As any seller whose account has been hacked would know, there is always a great loss. Sellers lose the faith from their customers; they can lose funds if their bank information is stolen; and they also lose potential income for the time they are not selling and working to resolve the issue. Unlike the Facebook suit, Amazon sellers are not subject to being tracked; they are subject to being deprived of their livelihood. Likewise, there is a level of reasonable expectation of privacy on the Amazon website. Sellers create accounts with added security measures to ensure their information is not stolen from them.

It is likely that Amazon sellers are more similar to the victims in the Anthem and Yahoo lawsuits. In the Yahoo case—the users were not warned of the security breach. Likewise, some Amazon sellers are not informed that their information has been hacked by Amazon; rather they discover this violation on their own. In the Anthem case, these people had their personal information exposed. Likewise, when a seller's account is hacked, their entire account is hacked. Their personal information, their bank information, and their listing information are exposed to the hacker.

FOURTH OF JULY SURPRISE FOR BIG-TIME SELLERS

Before and after July 4, 2017, Amazon brought a level of insecurity in the way they manage their business to third-party sellers. At Amazon Sellers Lawyer, we received countless calls from large companies who

---

44 Jonathan Stempel, *Facebook Beats Privacy Lawsuit in U.S. Over User Tracking*, Reuters, http://www.reuters.com/article/us-facebook-decision-idUSKBN19O1Q4 (last visited Aug. 10, 2017).

were kicked off of the platform due to intellectual property complaints. These large companies all had a few commonalities: they were large companies bringing in a substantial amount of revenue, and they all had multiple complaints against them, ranging from thirty complaints to fifty complaints.

All these companies received one final complaint, and that one complaint was the "straw that broke the camel's back." Whether it was an account with thirty-four complaints, and the thirty-fifth is what knocked them off, or forty-nine complaints, and the fiftieth is what knocked them off, it all occurred immediately before and immediately after the Fourth of July.

What is strange is that all these complaints were solely intellectual property violations. Multiple...sometimes dozens of intellectual property-right complaints. Amazon usually has a zero to no tolerance for IP complaints. For smaller businesses, it can be as little as one complaint that will knock them off. We see it time and time again; a complaint that may or may not be legitimate results in a seller losing his or her account. Why didn't the first thirty or forty complaints knock off these sellers? Perhaps Amazon treats the smaller third-party businesses differently than the third-party sellers who bring in a substantially larger profit.

We suspect that Amazon was trying out a new filter or algorithm that reviewed accounts after new complaints were asserted. This has been a common trend for Amazon.

Amazon periodically suspends accounts in large quantities during certain events. A recent mass suspending occurred during the last two weeks before the 2017 Super Bowl Weekend. Many third-party sellers who sold NFL items, regardless of whether they were selling authentic items, were suspended to combat counterfeits. The sellers were left suspended and needing to prove that their items were indeed authentic.

What we have concluded is that there are certain times when Amazon decides to send many suspensions. We saw it with NFL products around the Super Bowl, and now we have seen it with big companies around the Fourth of July. One account had over fifty complaints against them; however, we successfully had twelve of those complaints retracted. Those twelve retractions were enough for Amazon to reinstate the seller and allow the seller to return to his or her successful business. This raises a few questions: If Amazon can reinstate someone with twelve retractions but thirty-eight remained, what does that mean for the business with three complaints but can only remove one?

The plans of actions go beyond just retracted complaints. A good POA must have proper documentation, demonstrating that the items are not violating any IP rights and have documentation showing the items are authentic. This coupled with retractions will help the chances of Amazon reinstating that account. If a seller can show that the complaints are baseless, regardless of retraction, then that may be enough for Amazon. Additionally at Amazon Sellers Lawyer, our clients who have retained our services mention in their POA that they have hired a law firm to handle the issue. Showing initiative will also strengthen your POA. That is why it is so important to have invoices and use an authorized manufacturer to prove to Amazon that you are only in the business of selling authentic items that do not violate any IP rights.

Twelve

Accounts and Sellers Outside
of the United States

A mazon Sellers Lawyer has branched out and now has offices across
the globe: New York, London, Dublin, Shenzhen, and Mumbai. In the

United Kingdom, there are more stringent intellectual property laws than in the United States. Therefore, if you are a UK seller, it is important to be aware of the laws that apply to you. Remember, you may not be violating an Amazon policy, but you may be in violation of certain regulations.

In China, it seems that Amazon handles Chinese accounts differently than US accounts. Sellers who are physically located in mainland China have the same types of suspensions, but it seems that these accounts have been subject to stricter review. Our Shenzhen office manager, Cherish Mei stated that as a result of being more strict, it is harder for Chinese sellers. In situations where sellers are being treated unfairly, they are still able to arbitrate. This is why prevention is the best advice for sellers across the globe. It is easy to make careless mistakes, and those mistakes are not worth potentially losing your Amazon business.

There are also significant challenges that seem to make it harder for Amazon to identify sellers located in China that have multiple accounts.

- Amazon's Tracking of IP Addresses. In China, practically everyone uses VPNs to avoid the Chinese government's Great Firewall. It seems that the VPNs also serve to prevent Amazon from using IP addresses to catch sellers located in China selling through many accounts.
- Amazon's Bank Tracking. Unlike the United States, there are few banks in China. In addition, many sellers who are located in China use money-transferring services.
- Last Names. There are approximately ninety-five or so last names for over a billion people. This means that untold number of people selling on Amazon have similar names.
- Putting Accounts in Staff Members' Names. In China, the cost of staff is substantially lower than in the United States or Europe. An Amazon seller can easily have twenty to fifty employees at the same cost as five to ten would cost in the United States. Amazon

sellers located in China can use these staff members' names to open additional accounts.

WIPO

The World Intellectual Property Organization's (WIPO) website states that they are the "global forum for intellectual property services, policy, information and cooperation." Many sellers are unaware of the World Trade Organization. "The World Trade Organization administers the Agreement on Trade-Related Aspects of Intellectual Property Rights (TRIPS), which sets forth obligations related to intellectual property rights, including copyright and enforcement measures, in the context of a multilateral trade agreement."[45] These agreements are what allow creators across the globe the comfort of protections internationally.

As more sellers on Amazon create their private labels, their own products, designs, or inventions, Amazon sellers' needs for filing their own trademarks, copyright, patents, and so on continues to grow. While many American inventors are familiar with the IP process within the United States, they are not familiar with what is happening in other countries. Amazon reaches a customer base that is worldwide. That means, if you are selling your product on Amazon, it is going to be exposed to customers and infringers around the globe.

The United States has its own set of intellectual property protections, but they are limited to the United States. If an inventor files and is approved of Patent protection, then they are secured with that protection for twenty years. However, some sellers wish to gain protections on a global level. The International Patent System, Patent Cooperation Treaty (PCT) has 152 contracting states and is the office that assists other offices grant patents. In order to obtain protection, you would file an international patent application with the PCT. "The IP services that WIPO offers, such as the facilitation of international patent protection under the PCT

---

45 *International Copyright Relations of the United States*, copyright.gov, https://www.copyright.gov/circs/circ38a.pdf (last visited Aug. 10, 2017).

System, complement services available at the national and/or regional level. It's important to remember that WIPO does not actually grant patents per se; the grant or refusal of a patent still rests with the relevant national or regional patent office."[46]

Trademarks are also important to protect when running a business. "At the international level, you have two options: either you can file a trademark application with the trademark office of each country in which you are seeking protection, or you can use WIPO's Madrid System."[47] The Madrid system provided by WIPO provides protection in 114 countries.

---

46 *Frequently Asked Questions: Patents*, WIPO—World Intellectual Property Organization, http://www.wipo.int/patents/en/faq_patents.html (last visited Aug. 10, 2017).

47 *Trademarks*, WIPO—World Intellectual Property Organization, http://www.wipo.int/trademarks/en/ (last visited Aug. 10, 2017)

Thirteen

Getting Reinstated When Amazon Refuses to Reinstate: Taking the Decision out of Amazon's Hands

CJ's Side Note

Arbitration is a method of resolving disputes without going to court. If you sell on Amazon, you agreed to arbitrate any disputes with Amazon. Arbitration is generally faster and cheaper than litigation. Amazon insists on using the American Arbitration Association.

If you are thinking about suing or filing for arbitration against Amazon, I suggest that you first calm down and focus on your goal. Your goal should be getting back to business. Prior to arbitration, look at the built-in options: Plans of Action (numerous), writing to Policy Teams, writing to the Bezos Escalation Team, contacting Amazon's legal department, and then, if still no recourse, consider arbitration.

When pursuing the arbitration option, you should use a cost-benefit analysis. Is the cost of filing through arbitration worth the potential reward? If what you had lost is a small monetary amount, then arbitration may not be the best option.

Lately, there has been an increase in non-suspension-related issues that are worthy of arbitration or at least contacting the legal team. Amazon sellers are being subject to hacking and lost inventory. One option to resolve these issues is to first contact the legal team. Amazon Sellers Lawyer has been successful in communicating with the Amazon legal team to restore the accounts that have been stolen by hackers. Additionally, if Amazon loses a seller's inventory, it may be best to conduct communications with the legal team before going forward with arbitration.

When contacting the Amazon legal team, is it apparent that you show a timeline of the events that occurred. State specific dates—when was your account suspended, when and how many times have you created plans of actions. State that you have reached out to Jeff Bezos' team. Hiring an attorney to contact the legal team should only be done after you have exhausted all options. We at Amazon Sellers Lawyer have been able to successfully reinstate seller's accounts that otherwise would have been stuck in the endless cycle of plan of actions. The best way to avoid reaching this point is to create a comprehensive plan of action first. Many times plan of actions are rushed due to their short deadline, and sellers are forced to send multiple submissions, eventually needing to hire an attorney to contact the Amazon legal team. The best action is to be effective from the beginning.

If arbitration is your last option, there are multiple avenues to getting your claim heard. While you can request arbitration within your state, Amazon also allows telephonic hearings. More and more people are turning to arbitration when they have no option left, but an attorney must handle your claim. The attorney will be able to communicate on your behalf via phone or videoconference, making arbitration easily accessible when needed. When filing arbitration, you will need an attorney. At Amazon Sellers Lawyer, we cite Amazon's business solutions agreement (BSA) and file pursuant to this agreement if there has been a breach in the agreement.

THE ARBITRATION PROCESS

Demand for Arbitration. If you need to take the decision about reinstating your Amazon sellers' account out of Amazon's hands, then you draft a document called a Demand for Arbitration. This document is like the initial documents in a lawsuit: you must spell out the claim against Amazon. If you fail to include all of your claims or your Demand for Arbitration is unclear, you could lose the opportunity to argue those issues. Include your entire claim in your Demand for Arbitration.

The Demand for Arbitration must then be filed with the American Arbitration Association and "served" or provided to Amazon. Amazon's copy of the document must go to a specific address that Amazon has indicated for these types of documents.

Selection of an Arbitrator. After Amazon responds to your Demand for Arbitration, you will receive a list of arbitrators. You must number your top three choices in numerical order. Amazon's lawyers will receive the same list and they will also number their choices. You will receive the CVs of the arbitrators to help you decide who you want to choose.

Preliminary Conference. Every case will have a prehearing conference with the arbitrator. During the Preliminary Conference, you will provide the arbitrator with a synopsis of your claims. Amazon's lawyers will do the same. Then, a schedule for the exchange of documents and information will occur.

Hearing. Within about three (3) months of filing, you will have your hearing. About two weeks afterward, you will have your decision. Amazon seems to comply with the decisions whether they agree with the decisions or not.

Fourteen

Maintaining Your Business, Why Thinking Ahead Is Essential

A mazon knows their sellers are replaceable. That is why it is essential that prevention become a key aspect of running your business. This involves more than just following Amazon's rules. You must predict the Amazon's next move.

During the Super Bowl of 2016, Amazon increased their rate of suspensions with their sellers. Those Amazon sellers who were in the business of selling NFL items were kicked off the super-store, many times, without good cause. This was done in an effort to reduce the amount of counterfeit and inauthentic NFL items sold through the website. Unfortunately, many of the sellers who were suspended did not actually sell counterfeit or inauthentic items. They were grouped with those who disobeyed the law simply because of the item they sold. Those who had the invoices to support their defense of selling authentic, legal products were able to have their accounts reinstated. However, those who could not demonstrate that they had obtained their goods from an authorized manufacturer were not so lucky, despite selling authentic items. Why is this? Amazon is very specific as to what invoices they will deem to be adequate. That means your receipts and invoices from stores like Wal-Mart, Marshalls, or any other department store will not suffice.

"While buying from Wal-Mart [and selling the item on Amazon], is not against the rules, it's a dangerous game to be playing."
—Kerry McDonald, Managing Paralegal at Amazon Sellers Lawyer.

It is best to purchase your items from the actual manufacturer as a safe suit. If Amazon suspends your account, you will need to provide legitimate documentation. Amazon has begun moving toward preventative measures to protect major brands. They suspended people first, asked for proof of authenticity later. The NFL issue could happen again; it could be the next World Cup, or perhaps the next Olympics. As a seller, it is important to be vigilant. Maintaining your business in accordance to Amazon's rules is sometimes not enough. Make sure you have a back-up plan, make sure you have documentation proving authenticity for all of your items. This is your business, and thinking two steps ahead is essential.

BRAND REGISTRY 2.0

Amazon created Brand Registry as a tool to protect sellers. "Many sellers encounter problems maintaining their own listings. Once you are registered with brand registry, you obtain the rights to control the content for your private label products and listings within that registered brand."[48]

Working with Brand Registry allows sellers to manage their own product's listing. Sellers are able to format their listings accordingly. Sellers are provided the option to bold any sections that they choose on their description. Additionally, "this means that you will have control over your product's ID. You will be able to use a GCID (Global Catalog Identifier), assigned by Amazon, which can be used instead of UPCs."[49]

The original Brand Registry required sellers to file an application on the Seller Central account called, "Amazon Brand Registry Enrollment Request" and fill out the company's information. However, in May 2017, Amazon implemented an updated version of Brand Registry, Brand Registry 2.0. This is a fully unleashed update that has provided more tools for IP protection. While the Amazon upgrade is still under development, there is hope that this new version will benefit Amazon sellers. As of now, the system is used to protect sellers and their brands. Unfortunately, sellers are still having their listings hijacked. However, the perks of the new version include access to information such as a comprehensive list of all the brands that are registered.

There is a higher standard that needs to be met by sellers in order to be registered for Brand Registry 2.0. One change is that now sellers must prove they have a registered trademark. This means: sellers in the United States must file with the USPTO and receive legitimate rights to their brand. While it is possible to file a trademark on your own, applications are costly and take time for approval. It is in the best interest of your

---

48 C. J. Rosenbaum & Nicole Kulaga, Your Guide to Selling Fashion on Amazon.
49 Id.

company to hire a professional IP attorney to handle your application to make sure that it is correctly completed.

Once you have a registered trademark, you will need to file an application for Brand Registry 2.0. You will have to do this even if you were previously registered with Brand Registry if you want to be in the upgraded version. You will also need to demonstrate to Amazon that you have a registered trademark and you own the rights to that mark.

The Brand Registry allows sellers to have more control over their business. Sellers approved on Brand Registry 2.0 are able to search by image and brand name to detect if anyone is using their marks or brand name. Additionally, there is a direct link provided to sellers to report any infringement violations that are discovered. These updates are extremely beneficial to the entrepreneurs who wish to have their creative works protected on a platform that is subject to many intellectual property infringers. The new Brand Registry is still developing, but this extra level of security is needed to combat the growing number of infringers on the global website.

About C.J. Rosenbaum, Rosenbaum Famularo, P.C. and AmazonSellersLawyer. com

C.J. Rosenbaum founded Rosenbaum Famularo, P.C., the law firm behind AmazonSellersLawyer.com. The law firm that helps sellers across the globe. Our clients have the opportunity to meet with us, in person, at locations in California, Seattle, New York, London, Ireland, Shenzhen, India, and the United Kingdom. The firm provides Amazon Suspension Services, assistance in obtaining the retraction of intellectual property complaints, consultations for law firms, legal opinions and other services for Amazon sellers. Each client has his or her own unique needs. Our team has the experience needed to analyze your situation, your business, and work with you to get your Amazon sellers' account reinstated.

As an Amazon Seller, your e-commerce success depends on your cooperation with the rules and regulations set by Amazon. When you are conducting an online business through Amazon, an account suspension brings your entire operation to a halt. Amazon Seller Suspensions can happen at any time—even with just one complaint from a buyer.

Amazon Sellers don't need to live in fear of policy violations, buyer complaints, and account suspensions any longer. Amazon Sellers now have a lawyer on their side.

Sellers don't need to worry about their private information being revealed: with a law firm helping you with your Plans of Action and other needs, your information is protected by the attorney-client privilege.

Table of Authorities

- 17 U.S.C.S. § 512
- 15 U.S.C. § 1127.
- 15 U.S.C. § 1051.
- Amazon.com, Forum Moderator.
- Amazon Law Library.
- *Amazon.com's Third-Party Sellers Hit by Hackers*, Fox Business (2017), http://www.foxbusiness.com/markets/2017/04/10/amazon-coms-third-party-sellers-hit-by-hackers.html (last visited Aug. 10, 2017).
- Anna Aria et al., *Class Action Settlement on Its Way: Vail v. Yahoo! Lawsuit Filed*, Consumer Law Mag. (2017), http://consumerlawmagazine.com/vail-v-yahoo-lawsuit/ (last visited Aug. 10, 2017).
- *Anthem Agrees to $115 Million Settlement of Data Breach Lawsuit*, Fox Business (2017), http://www.foxbusiness.com/features/2017/06/23/anthem-agrees-to-115-million-settlement-data-breach-lawsuit.html (last visited Aug. 10, 2017).
- Appistry, Inc. v. Amazon.com, Inc., No. 4:13CV2547, 2015 U.S. Dist. LEXIS 24421 (E.D. Mo. Mar. 2, 2015).
- *Categories and Products Requiring Approval*, Amazon.com Help: Categories and Products Requiring Approval, https://www.amazon.com/gp/help/customer/display.html/?nodeId=14113001 (last visited Aug. 10, 2017).

- Christian Louboutin S.A. v. Yves Saint Laurent Am. Holding, Inc., 696 F.3d 206 (2d Cir. N.Y. 2012).
- C. J. Rosenbaum & Nicole Kulaga, Your Guide to Selling Fashion on Amazon.
- *Condition Guidelines*, Amazon.com Help: Condition Guidelines, https://www.amazon.com/gp/help/customer/display.html?nodeId=1161242 (last visited Aug. 10, 2017).
- *Community Guidelines*, Amazon.com Help: Profile & Community Guidelines.
- *Conditions of Use*, Amazon.com Help: Conditions of Use, https://www.amazon.com/gp/help/customer/display.html/ref=ap_frn_condition_of_use?ie=UTF8&nodeId=508088 (last visited Aug. 10, 2017).
- Debra Weinstein, *Note, Defining Expeditious: Uncharted Territory of The DMCA Safe Harbor Provision: A Survey of What We Know and Do Not Know About the Expeditiousness of Service Provider Responses to Takedown Notifications*, 26 Cardozo Arts & Ent L.J. 589 (2008).
- Digital Millennium Copyright Act of 1998, 17 U.S.C. § 512 (2016).
- Duraco Products Inc. v. Joy Plastic Enterprises Ltd., 40 F.3d 1431 (3d Cir. 1994).
- Ellison v. Robertson, 357 F.3d 1072, 1076 (9th Cir. 2004).
- *FBA Prohibited Products*, Amazon.com Help: FBA Prohibited Products, https://www.amazon.com/gp/help/customer/display.html?nodeId=201790610 (last visited Aug. 10, 2017)
- *Frequently Asked Questions: Patents*, WIPO—World Intellectual Property Organization, http://www.wipo.int/patents/en/faq_patents.html (last visited Aug. 10, 2017).
- *How Long Does Patent, Trademark or Copyright Protection Last?*, stopfakes.gov, https://www.stopfakes.gov/article?id=How-Long-Does-Patent-Trademark-or-Copyright-Protection-Last (last visited Aug. 10, 2017).

- *Inside WIPO*, WIPO—World Intellectual Property Organization, http://www.wipo.int/about-wipo/en/ (last visited Aug. 10, 2017).
- Jeffrey Milstein, Inc. v. Greger, Lawlor, Roth, Inc., 58 F.3d 27, 31 (2d Cir. 1992).
- John H. Harland Co. v. Clarke Checks, Inc., 771 F.2d 966, 980 (11th Cir. 1983), cited with approval in Two Pesos, Inc. v. Taco Cabana, Inc., 505 U.S. 763, 112 S.Ct. 2753 (1992).
- Jonathan Stempel, *Facebook Beats Privacy Lawsuit in U.S. Over User Tracking*, Reuters, http://www.reuters.com/article/us-facebook-decision-idUSKBN19O1Q4 (last visited Aug. 10, 2017).
- Leegin Creative Leather Prods. v. PSKS, Inc., 551 U.S. 877, 881 (U.S. 2007).
- Margaret Cronin Fisk, *Yahoo Failed to Protect Consumers from Hacking, Lawsuit Says*, Bloomberg.com (2016), https://www.bloomberg.com/news/articles/2016-12-15/yahoo-failed-to-protect-consumers-from-hacking-lawsuit-says (last visited Aug. 10, 2017).
- Milo & Gabby, LLC v. Amazon.com, No. C12-1932RSM, 2015 U.S. Dist. LEXIS 149939 (W.D. Wash. Nov. 3, 2015).
- *Packaging and Prep Requirements*, Amazon.com Help: Packaging and Prep Requirements, https://www.amazon.com/gp/help/customer/display.html/?nodeId=200243250#packaging (last visited Aug. 10, 2017).
- Robert Segall, E-Commerce, Amazon, and the DMCA: Fighting Copyright Bullying in the Modern E-Commerce Context.
- *Trade Dress: The Forgotten Trademark Right*, Findlaw, http://corporate.findlaw.com/intellectual-property/trade-dress-the-forgotten-trademark-right.html (last visited Aug. 10, 2017).
- *Trademarks*, WIPO—World Intellectual Property Organization, http://www.wipo.int/trademarks/en/ (last visited Aug. 10, 2017).
- Trade Secret, *Black's Law Dictionary* (10th ed. 2014).
- Two Pesos, Inc. v. Taco Cabana, Inc., 505 U.S. 763, 765 n.1, 112 S.Ct. 2755, 2755 n.1 (1992).
- Weinstein, *supra* note 3.

- *What is Trade Dress?*, www.nolo.com, http://www.nolo.com/legal-encyclopedia/what-trade-dress.html (last visited Aug. 10, 2017).
- *Yahoo Class Action—Privacy Breach Class Action Lawsuit*, Yahoo! Privacy Breach Class Action, http://www.yahooprivacybreach.com/ (last visited Aug. 10, 2017).